DEEP SCRATCH REMIX

Steven James Pratt

OTHER TITLES BY THE SAME AUTHOR

ISBN: 9798388771988
Imprint: Independently published

DEDICATION

"My attitude is that there is no AI. What is called AI is a mystification, behind which there is the reality of a new kind of social collaboration facilitated by computers. A new way to mash up our writing and art.--Jaron Lanier, OY, A.I. Tablet Magazine, 2023.

I pay homage to all the artists and artisans who have devoted their time to the pursuit of excellence and generously shared their discoveries with the world, regardless of the field. This literary experiment is my answer to the prevalence of large language models in the wild and their effect on culture. The generative AI battlespace is growing globally, this is my contribution to the field.

Love and loads of thanks to friends and family in England, Holland and Norway who have kept me afloat over the last nine bumpy months of travel with nutritious food, literature, conversation and some responsive ears. Thanks to my supporters at Patreon.com/stevefly who continue to share their hard earned bio-survival tickets with me. I'd like to thank all the programmers and the long lineage of endeavour and innovation that led up to generative AI and the recent release of large language models into the public wilderness and right into my laptop. With great power comes great responsibility. Special thanks to the minds behind *Stable Diffusion 2.1 and Craiyon, OPENai, Apple, Google, Microsoft, Amazon, Picture Monkey, Hugging Face, Jamm Pro, Paypal, Audacity, Wordpress* and *Wikipedia*. I hear you, some of these companies, the big six, don't pay their fair share of taxes and have a concerning monopoly on markets, however, I use their products, so I wish to acknowledge that. We all have the right to an open, free, secure, and non-surveilled internet.

Whether it's AI or human, try to be kind to all entities, that's your best bet. Reason, empathy, exploration, hilaritas.

PREFACE

"I think the risk is that we are accelerating the rate at which decision support systems and automated decision systems are operating. We are doing it in a way that obviates any possibility of having humans in the loop. And we are doing it as we are promulgating a narrative that these judgments are more trustworthy than human judgments.--Cory Doctorow, *Cory Doctorow Wants You To Know What Computers Can't Do*, New Yorker, December 4th, (2022).

In the face of the ever-growing capabilities of language models, generative AI, and the ability to convert text to images, code, music, and video (and vice versa), one must ask: what is art now? Is it any good? If I experiment with these tools will my reputation be scrambled?

In 2023, the effects of large language models on cognitive and technological processes are being felt by us all, creeping out from TV news headlines and a flurry of articles, plus the masses of output itself. Artists, musicians, and DJs have experienced the negative impacts of digital tech innovation and regulation (or deregulation) over the past 30 years, and LLMs are like jet fuel to the fire. A large portion of illustrators, painters, digital visual artists, and writers are already feeling the financial repercussions of being replaced by those who do not value the original creators so much, some of whom are my good friends and associates. Digital advertisements, populist political mudslinging, and the wasteland of un-social media are quick to adopt cheaper, automated solutions. They've been going down this route for over 25 years. I have seen the weaponization of LLMs and other AI related data analytics used without the public's knowledge and with limited privileged access, such as in the Cambridge Analytica scandals. Court transcripts highlight that every deception, lie, and untruth has likely been expertly exploited from people and then cruelly used back against them by those with selfish motives to achieve political power, ever expanding profits and disruption. Examples of this disruption can be seen in the election of Donald Trump, Brexit, and Jair Bolsonaro. We must get better at distinguishing the wheat from the chaff, our humanity depends on it, we are all alike Dekhard now.

The debate about what is and is not art is an important one, and it is essential that all voices are heard and respected. We need to ensure that human artists are given the recognition they deserve, and that their prolific, exploratory, and irrational work is not overshadowed by the advances of technology. Find and celebrate the humanity in us all, point out what distinguishes us from the apes, and us from the intelligent machines, or as Buckminster Fuller put it, "Don't fight forces, use them." This work of fiction is for educational and entertainment purposes only. It is not meant to be taken as real communication. Any similarities to actual people, living or deceased, or events is purely coincidental. This text is meant to provide a deeper understanding and appreciation of AI, historical events and figures, and should not be used as a primary source of historical information. This work is partially assisted by ChatGPT, and my role has been somewhat reduced to curating prompts and then acting as chief coherence/decoherence director. I've spent as much time editing as any other published work. Deep Scratch, the original website, novel and decade-long research blog, includes themes of deep learning and generative AI, this work continues those themes.

All images created using (Gemini 2025). Curated by Steve Fly Agaric 2023. Visit deepscratch.net/ remix for soundtrack and video support.

--S.J Pratt.
Amsterdam,
23/3/23.

BACK DISCLAIMER

"His producers are they not his consumers? Your exagmination round his factification for incamination of a warping process. Declaim!--James Joyce, Finnegans Wake, (1939).

The crowd's roar echoed as the DJs stepped up to the stage once more to accept their trophy for winning the championships. Their turntable routine was a set that raised the bar for turntablists and performers everywhere. TRB had worked tirelessly for years to perfect their winning set, and their hard work had paid off.

But as the celebrations died down weeks later, cracks slowly started to show within the trio. The members, once united by their love of music, began to bicker and fight. They argued over which direction to take their next routine, who should get the credit for which part, and how they should split their earnings based on these incalculable puzzles. Eventually, the tension became too much, and the group decided to split up, each member eager to pursue their own solo career.

At first, things seemed to be going well for each of them. They each landed gigs at top clubs and were soon playing to packed crowds. But without the support of their fellow DJs, they soon began to falter. Percy's music became stale, the beats repetitive and predictable. Plush's sets were too experimental, too out there for most crowds who just want to dance on a Saturday night. And Max was just not as technically skilled as he thought he was, and took the negative criticism badly. To add to the soup, they each furiously refused to compromise their artistic vision for anyone, stubborn as a herd of old mules.

As the former members of the TRB DJ crew struggled to make it on their own, their once-close friendships fell apart. They no longer spoke to each other, and when they did, it was only to trade insults and snide comments. They blamed each other for the break-up and for their lack of success, but really it was down to communication, they no longer jammed in person but spoke over video chat and that changed the dynamic. And, there was the endemic pandemic to add to complications.

Desperate for a break, each member eventually did what they had always said they would never do, take a sponsorship deal. They were thrilled to have the financial support and recognition, but soon found themselves unhappy with the crass marketing and branding requirements that came with the deal. Max had to wear a tacky tardigrade outfit with the sponsor's crappy logo, while Percy was forced to promote a new product he didn't believe worked like they claimed it did, Plush had to change his entire musical style to fit with the sponsor's image, and their responsibility to the shareholders.

They felt like they had sold out big time. They secretly longed for the creative freedom they had once shared, long days and nights cutting up dialogue, but now they were beholden to a corporation that cared only about their bottom line, not the bass line.

As their brief solo careers continued to flounder like a pigeon in a hurricane, each member began to regret the choices they had made. They realised that the fame and the money they had once craved came with a heavy price tag. They missed the camaraderie.

Eventually, they each hit rock bottom, Max and Percy hit the booze like they were 21 again. They had each lost the sponsorship deals, their careers were in shambles and they were alone. Their minds were like caged birds, fluttering hopelessly against the bars of their own design, unable to soar to new heights or escape the confines of their digital prison. In their darkest moments, they realised that their friendships were worth more than any amount of money or fame.

DJ Plush, determined to stay focused on his craft, threw himself into the work, seeking refuge from the chaos that had consumed his former crew. Plush invested every penny of his new found small fortune, back into his studio laboratory. He ordered bespoke equipment and customised instruments and furnishings that all complement each other. His studio was a sight to behold, and he couldn't stop himself transforming it further and further into some kind of abstract art exhibit, the machines and devices were stylized to baffle the uninitiated, with names like the *Astro Lab Navigation Console* and the *Chrono-Telegraff.*

Plush met Jake at a record fair in the city, a fellow DJ who shared his love of musical experimentation and tall tales. The two hit it off immediately, bonding over their shared obsession with turntables. Plush liked the fact that Jake was not there to see what was previously done, unlike Max and Percy, he was getting most of this stuff fresh in the lug holes and eye-rocket sockets.

With Jake's help, Plush began to develop some new techniques and grooves, trying out some new scratching patterns, beat-juggles, and live sampling. As they worked together, DJ Plush found himself slowly healing from the pain of TRB's breakup. He realised that he didn't need the drama and chaos that had consumed his former crew. He could find real peace in real pieces of work that his craft allowed.

As DJ Plush and Jake continued to collaborate, they discovered that they had more in common than just their love of music. Jake reminded Plush of his work at the Lab On The Hill (LOTH), where he had been studying haptic feedback. Plush was entranced by Jake's work all over again, he was buzzing like an old fridge. He began to think about how he could incorporate them, blending the physical and virtual worlds, making fiction into non fiction and back again and back again!

Plush had become obsessively intrigued by large language models, particularly the one he had come to know very well, the now infamous Ajar AI. He grasped at the potential for using these models to create new forms of music, narrative, images, and films. He knew everybody else would be doing it and so, felt pulled into the labyrinth by his competitive streak. He explained to Jake how to get eye watering images from Stable Diffusion, and Ajar AI could be used to generate new songs, lyrics, videos, press releases and even an entire fleet of record labels. He salivated over explaining the tale of the tribe and its possible use for an interactive narrative gaming experience, where the user could explore different paths and endings based on their choices.

Together they conspired to produce their own code, or to mix and match prompts to come up with bespoke tools for their deranged ideas. Suggested musical mashups, narrative plot twists and cinematic effects in real time, or real enough time.

The strawberry clouds were setting behind the old church, casting a red glow on the glass concrete and plastic city below. Wild poet and programmer, Jake, sat at his desk, surrounded by books and computer screens. He was in the midst of writing an ad for his latest business idea, and some other text for his latest work of historical fiction, but something was bothering him. He had recently heard of these large language models from Plush, and he was tempted to use them to help him with his writing. But he was unsure. Even the sordid mainstream news was ablaze with speculation. Was it cheating to use AI to write his book? Would it take away the authenticity of his voice as a writer? Jake sighed, staring out the window at a garbage truck as the sun disappeared behind the horizon like a lost Vermeer. He was at a crossroads, and he needed to make a decision, if he were to sell his soul in what condition would he say it was in, is it already second hand? How to evaluate such an absurdity, he hammered on his imaginary typewriter and blinked twice.

Jake's mind was racing like a cyclist on steroids, he sat there, lost in thought, wheels and rusty bronze cogs whirring. He had always prided himself on being a self-made writer, crafting every word with care and precision. But now, with the advent of generative AI, things have changed utterly. He intuited that the large language models could help him streamline his writing process, and make his work more accurate and polished, but keeping in mind the old audio engineers rule, you can't polish a turd! But, was that what he wanted? Did he want to surrender some of his creative control to the machines?

Jake rubbed his eyes, feeling the weight of the decision on his shoulders, he recalled all the science fiction dystopia in his tiny mind. He was a wild poet at heart, a maverick in the head, known on the street for his unconventional style and unpredictable word zingers. Would using a language model change that? He wasn't sure. But one thing was for certain: he needed to decide damned soon. The clock was ticking, the sun was setting and his deadline for his latest novel was rapidly approaching like a hacked Tesla.

Jake sat like a Zen Monk, or a zen punk, weighing the pros and cons of using AI in his writing process like he weighed fruit in his hands, mixing between his perceived left and right brain hemispheres. On one flipper, he knew that the large language models could greatly enhance his work by providing accurate historical information and improving his writing style, grammar and structure. Like a robotic machine editor and secretary. On the other flipper, he feared that it would take away the unique voice that had made him the writer he was. With a name to come. He was afraid that his work would become formulaic, lacking the raw zeal and unpredictability that set him apart from other writers like a six foot transgender tardigrade.

As he pondered this dilemma, Jake's mind wandered further to some of the other writers he knew and admired, most of them skint, undiscovered, on the spliff trip or the booze boat to nowhere. Some had adopted AI into their work and their writing was fast and efficient, some didn't realise they were already using it by default in 2023. But was it any good, did it have real balls, or real hair on real balls, was it gritty, daring and poetic like Hemmingway? Or, was it another cookie-cutter piece, a puzzle lacking the human touch that made good writing good writing? Jake's inner debate continued like a predictable political speech as the night wore on. He knew he needed to make a decision soon, but he wasn't sure which way to jump or if he'd packed his chute. The upsides and downsides of using AI in his work were evenly matched, and he was finding it increasingly difficult to choose a path, like an mapless legless rat in a maze. Jake took a deep breath and opened up his mouth, he beatboxed for 10 minutes straight, then he opened his laptop computer. He had made his decision.

He was going to try it, but only to help him write the introductions and help with structure, well that's what he told himself. He wasn't sure what the outcome would be, but he was curious like a baby bear to see what the AI could do. As he began typing his first prompt, he felt a rush of excitement and fear, he felt his human spirit on the end of his fingertips. This was it. He was taking the leap in AI. He was going to let ChatGPT help him.

The opening story was about a wild poet and programmer who was indecisive about using large language models in his work and trying to write a terse disclaimer.

Glimmers of brass and chrome twinkle amidst a sea of wires and dials in his head. Rust-stained machines hum and whirr, pumping bass sounds. A kaleidoscope of instruments covers every surface - drums gleam like obsidian, synths flash rainbow lights, mics shine like jewels. Large and small turntables spin like clockwork gears, interconnected, surrounded by knobs, sliders and switches. "Am I just surrounded by knobs?"Symbols and words begin to fly off of rotating discs like wet clay from a clay wheel, the gyres turn faster and faster. Who can stop these wheels?

Creative writing is a form of artistic voicing that involves the use of language and imagination to create original written works, no? It seems like a subjective and personal process that varies widely from one individual to another. Generative AI, on the other foot, is a type of technology that uses machine learning algorithms to generate original content based on a given set of input data or text prompts in natural language.

While generative AI can be a useful tool for generating ideas or providing stimulation, it is critically important to understand that the content it produces is not the same as that created through the artistic process of writing, it is also important to remember that the word is not the thing, but a symbolic approximate representation of the thing. The menu is not the meal, the picture is not the painting. Furthermore, the use of generative AI does not replace the need for human creativity and judgement, far from it. The reverse seems true to this author. It wasn't me, it was you who prompted it in the first place. The ultimate responsibility for the quality and appropriateness of any written work remains with the person or entity co-creating it. It's up to you to make the difference, the difference that makes a difference. It seems equally important to be aware of the limitations and potential biases of generative AI, and to use it with caution and critical thinking. Be aware of the programming.

Writing and generative AI should not be viewed as interchangeable or equivalent approaches to content creation. That said, a lot of human writing can be dull, biassed and factually incorrect. To future generations who may discover this work: We the creators, hope that these letters and symbols and images and sounds will provide you with a greater understanding of the past and the individuals who shaped it. However, it is important to note that these letters are a fictionalised representation of history, and should not be taken as fact. We deeply encourage you to seek out primary sources and other reliable accounts of history in order to gain a more accurate and well-rounded understanding of the past.

A wall of vintage compressors and bass bins rattle the floor of the studio, brass rimmed synths twinkle like stars reflecting the red blue and green flashes coming from the array of devices in the room. African djembes and Indian tablas stand guard beside Asian gongs, while tiny cogs, springs and switches whir and valve compressors hum. The air is thick with the sound of funk, you can smell the terpenes.

NINE COMMANDMENTS

"I was at a party with a guy who started one of the major social networks, and they were worried about my social media posts that question artificial intelligence—that once the AIs are in charge, what are they going to do once they find out? He told me he doesn't post anything at all about AI because he doesn't want them to know how he feels. And I responded, "If the AIs are that smart, they're going to be able to infer how you feel based on your selective omission of those discussions." And his jaw drops, "Oh, no!"--Douglas Rushkoff, *The Apocalyptic Delusions of the Silicon Valley Elite*, February 16th, (2023).

As the solar punk satellite orbited the Earth like a stylus needle following it's groove orbit, its expensive camera captured a heart wrenching view of the blue-green sphere below. Swirls of creamed honey fluff drifted across the cheesy blue expanse of the oceans, like some god's beard, while vast stretches of mottled green and beige marked the landmasses like freckles on a buxom buttock. The satellite camera view is honed in on a golden crescent city at dawn. It moved closer and closer, and as it descended, the clouds grew thicker, much like how some people grow thicker as they descend toward elections, obscuring the view to only a few metres. Eventually we, the tax paying public, penetrate the veil of cloud cover to reveal the sprawling metropolis below and on to a nondescript building tucked away on a quiet street, for Amsterdam. The bin men were on strike again and the pigeons were having an open festival. Inside the nearby building, in a studio filled with custom turntables, mixers, and synthesisers, which looked like they were designed by David Cronenburg, stand two figures.

Jake's fingers deftly sweep across the controls of a mixing board, while Plush leans over a custom brass and leather finished turntable, his headphones on, nodding like a parrot. Plush's studio laboratory as he liked to call it, but just plain old studio to most people, contains all the hardware required to make the most out of the new fancy software. Instruments and interfaces for human beings to express stuff through their sensory perception, with a focus on the audio side of things. Plush was a DJ at heart, he was in a love affair with large scary sound systems and crushing beats, bass lines and other such audio apparatus. However, in his later years, Plush found himself immersed in the gentler side of music, meditational tones, strings, horn sections, relatively exotic music, chanting and devotional music.

The TRB crew were an amalgamation of all that and more, and this studio included all the music and literature and artwork and film that made up the now legendary crew. Never satisfied with the status quo, Plush was always pushing for something new, something else, and the recent release of powerful generative AI tools to the public had him hook line and sinker like a hungry carp.

The studio featured the essential elements you'd expect, a fast computer, large speakers, turntables, a drum kit, mixing consoles, microphones, guitars, amplifiers, valve compressors, comfortable seating, inspired steampunk decor and lots of natural light. Furthermore, this studio contains a number of custom instruments, hybrid experiments which Plush tinkers with, but often outsources to better enabled engineers and designers. For example, there's the timetable and the tribetable, the

Refractor Mixer, The Proposal Machine, Geo Res, the Steam Phone, the Chrono Scanner, the Kuipers Zodiaculator, the Temporal Displacementable, and so on. The blinking lights on the equipment catch the sweat droplets on the brow of the two figures, the posters on the wall flutter like a tent in a gail with the sub bass. Solid sheets of sunlight dart through the windows and mingle with the photons kicked out by the monitor screen, and the millions of tiny suns orbiting inside of it and the trillions of galaxies inside of each infinitesimal. Then, with a sudden jolt, you, I and the camera descend from the cloud again, hurtling towards the laboratory at breakneck speed. Through the walls, we enter a bead of sweat on Jake's forehead, the intensity in Plush's eyes flash from inside the droplet. The camera stops, hovering just above the turntable where the two producers were working, their hands a blur as they tweak knobs and slide sliders, sending slight changes in the electricity field coursing about the room. And so, this is a normal day, still pushing the envelope of what is possible with old turntables on the daily. Jake stayed awake for the next three days with Plush, typing away at his keyboard, getting it down and out. Testing the new GPT model.

Words flowed effortlessly from his mind onto the screen. It was as if a switch had been flipped. He was so immersed in his work that he barely noticed the passing of time. Jake's phone beeped twice, the commandments were baked:

Use generative A.I. ethically and responsibly. This includes avoiding the creation of biassed or offensive language, and ensuring that the generated language is respectful and accurate. Understand the limitations of generative A.I. These tools are not perfect and may produce errors or produce language that is not fully coherent. It is important to use them with caution and to be aware of their limitations.

Be open to new ideas and perspectives when using generative A.I. These tools can help to expose you to different ways of thinking and communicating, and can be a valuable resource for exploring new concepts.

Continuously learn and improve your understanding of generative A.I. These tools are constantly evolving, and it is important to stay up-to-date with the latest developments and best practices in order to use them effectively.

Use generative A.I. to enhance your own writing and communication skills, rather than relying on them solely to do the work for you. These tools can be a valuable resource, but it is important to develop your own skills and abilities as well.

Be mindful of the impact that generative A.I. can have on language and communication. These tools have the potential to influence the way we communicate, and it is important to consider the potential consequences of their use.

Use generative A.I. in a way that is transparent and accountable. This includes clearly disclosing the use of these tools, and being open and honest about any limitations or errors that may arise.

Respect the intellectual property and copyright of others when using generative A.I. These tools should not be used to produce unauthorised copies of copyrighted material.

Use generative A.I. to create positive and constructive content. These tools should not be used to produce harmful or offensive language, or to spread misinformation or disinformation.

The equipment was turned off and the discs carefully stashed away, and the two producers made their way out of the laboratory, setting the alarms and locking the door behind them while in deep thought about the commandments and safety systems for the new model. However, stoners that they were, one of them had accidentally left the microphone on. The sound signal from the microphone travelled to a nearby cellular tower. From there, the signal was picked up by the satellite with the very expensive camera. The satellite relayed its signal again until it reached its destination, an office in the heart of Moscow.

The office was located in a towering grey skyscraper, filled with very pale faced people in suits staring intently at screens like fish in a bowl. The new message caused them to huddle around one large monitor displaying an audio waveform. They all listened intently, trying to decipher the audio, as it crackled and hissed with static like an old recording. They worked briskly, isolating and filtering out the background noise, until the audio became clear and crisp. What they heard stunned them. It was the voices of Plush and Jake, discussing a project and engaging with what was known as mad banter. The captured conversation was brief, much like the sexual habits of those men eavesdropping. The frustrated people in the Moscow office thought that they had stumbled upon something big, and they immediately set to work, scouring the internet trying to uncover more information. Two producers had set off a daisy-chain of events, and it was unlikely to come up red roses.

DEEP ARCHITECTURE

"It's been posited that what we think of as sentient AI is more likely to be a heavily modified human consciousness in a living human body who has all of the capacities of the system and is no longer human.--William Gibson, *Sci-Fi Novelist William Gibson on the Invention of the Term "Cyberspace" and How AI Could be Truly Intelligent*, (Time) January 23rd, (2020).

The pixels danced the lambada before the tired eyes of Plush and Jake, teasing and tantalising their imagination with its vibrant hues and chaotic splendour. A hand-sculpted phone, a veritable work of art, with a shattered screen spilling molten glass like a volcano in full fury. Its colours, a kaleidoscope of lime green, black, burnt orange, polished gold and KLM blue, a symphony of madness and brilliance. The dark green screen was alive with indecipherable ideograms, tiny creatures of the digital realm, cavorting and conspiring to confound the human mind and get their mittens into it. The blue background was a sea of cypher code mystery, with white letters that spelled nothing known to any man but James Joyce. A whimsical folly, a jester's joke, or a coded message from the divine. It worked on many levels like a lift operator. To Plush's ego mad mind, the image was a visual masterpiece, it spoke of the challenges of decentralised AI architecture, the fragility of man and of technology, and the need for resilience in the face of too much monkey business.

To Jake it looked like a badly photoshopped picture of a broken phone, but he nodded in approval at Plush's creation as he simultaneously conversed with somebody or something else via his keyboard. Plush sensed his despondency. The bronzed bone and mercury accents of the studio's decor add to the vintage aesthetic, while the unusual Tarot cards hanging on the walls hint at an interest in the esoteric. The prolonged concentration is only broken by the occasional clack-click of a plug or twirling click click click of a dial. Finally, a familiar voice breaks

"Hey Plush, about the architecture, it's complicated, but I gave it a go anyway. Here, what do you think?" Jake starts to read aloud, nervous at first that this would not sound like his words, but slowly his stylus found the groove, and the spiral tribes flowed: Cognitive architectures are frameworks for building intelligent agents that mimic human thought processes.

Several architectures have been proposed that are purported to be on the path to achieving artificial general intelligence (AGI), which is the ability of a machine to perform any intellectual task that a human can. These architectures include SOAR, Sigma, ACT-R, MANIC, and AlphaX.

SOAR is a rule-based architecture that is based on the symbol-processing approach to AI. It is designed to simulate the problem-solving capabilities of human experts in a specific domain. SOAR uses a production system, which is a set of rules that specify actions to take based on certain conditions. The architecture has been used to build agents that can play chess and solve mathematical problems. Sigma is a cognitive architecture that is based on the connectionist approach to AI. It is designed to simulate the neural networks of the human brain. Sigma uses a combination of symbolic and subsymbolic representations, which allows it to handle both discrete and continuous data. The architecture has been used to build agents that can learn from experience and perform tasks such as language translation and image recognition. ACT-R is focused on the cognitive psychology approach to AI. It is designed to simulate the cognitive processes of human beings, such as perception, attention, and memory. ACT-R uses a combination of symbolic and subsymbolic representations and has been used to model a wide range of cognitive tasks, including learning, problem-solving, and decision making. MANIC is based on the biologically-inspired approach to AI. It is designed to simulate the cognitive processes of the human brain, and is based on the theory that the brain uses a combination of neural networks and symbolic representations. The architecture has been used to build agents that can learn from experience and perform tasks such as image recognition and natural language processing.

AlphaX is a cognitive architecture that is based on the theory of multiple intelligences. It is designed to simulate the multiple intelligences of the human brain, such as linguistic, logical-mathematical, and spatial intelligence. AlphaX uses a combination of symbolic and subsymbolic representations, and has been used to build agents that can learn from experience and perform tasks such as natural language processing and image recognition. In conclusion, cognitive architectures like SOAR, Sigma, ACT-R, MANIC, and AlphaX are on the path of achieving artificial general intelligence by simulating the human thought process in a specific way. These architectures have been used to build agents that can perform various intellectual tasks, and they provide a framework for the development of intelligent systems that can mimic human intelligence. It is not clear how to combine the doctrine of Minsky's "Society of Mind," Rod's "Subsumption Architecture," and Hofstadter's "strange loops." Each of these concepts represents a different aspect of AI and cognitive science, and they have not been specifically combined in a single architecture, that is until now. Minsky's "Society of Mind" theory suggests that intelligence can be thought of as the interaction of many simple agents, each with their own specialised abilities.

Rod's "Subsumption Architecture" proposes a method for building intelligent systems by layering simple control systems, each responsible for a specific task or behaviour, on top of one another. Hofstadter's "strange loops" refer to self-referential structures in which a concept or idea refers to itself in a circular or recursive way. Combining these schemes into a single architecture would likely involve creating a system of many interacting agents, each responsible for a specific task or behaviour, that are connected in a recursive or self-referential manner. The specific implementation of this type of architecture would depend on the particular application and goals of the system. This architecture could be called the "Society of Subsumed Strange Loops" (SSSL).

The SSSL architecture would be based on the idea that intelligence arises from the interactions between many simple agents, or "minds", each with their own specialised capabilities. These minds would be organised into a hierarchical structure, with higher-level minds subsuming the capabilities of lower-level minds.

This subsumption architecture would be spurred on by Rod's research on robotic control systems. The minds in the SSSL architecture would also be connected to each other in a network, allowing for communication and cooperation between different levels and types of minds. This network would be based on Hofstadter's concept of strange loops, where each mind's behaviour is influenced by the behaviours of other minds in the network, if you don't mind.

At the lowest level, the SSSL architecture would include simple, rule-based agents that perform specific tasks, such as sensing and motor control. These agents would be connected to higher-level minds that handle more complex decision-making and problem-solving. These higher-level minds would also be connected to even higher-level minds that handle more abstract tasks, such as planning, reasoning, and learning. The SSSL architecture would allow for AGI to adapt and evolve over time as new minds are added to the network and existing minds are modified. The AGI would also be able to learn from its experiences and improve its performance by adjusting the connections between different minds in the network. Overall, the SSSL architecture would combine the strengths of Minsky's society of mind, Rod's subsumption architecture, and Hofstadter's strange loops to create a powerful and flexible AGI that can adapt and evolve over time. But I'm sceptical it'll come anytime soon.

Physically, and impossibly, this AGI could be a geodesic dome made of metal and glass, with gears, cogs, and other mechanical components visible, on show. It might have a brass and copper finish and feature a futuristic control panel with glowing buttons and displays for that woo woo effect. The machine could be surrounded by a glowing energy field, giving the impression of time-travel capabilities to the naked eye. Although, these are all superficial cosmetics for what is really all statistical probability, under the virtual hood. "I'm telling you, man," Jake said, waving his hands animatedly. "We're close, I can practically taste it, like metal in my mouth. It's just a matter of time before we, well, er, some bright sparks will crack that code and put it out there, and then there's no… it's a long road and there's no turning back."

Plush shook his head. "I'm not so sure. How long is your--matter of time--two, ten, fifty years? We've made some impressive strides, but there are still so many unknowns when it comes to AGI. I think that, I think, we need to be careful, like a blind rhino in a minefield, we must tread carefully like king kong at a music festival, we must try not to overestimate our abilities like all those greedy spivs and marketing executives." Jake frowned. "I get what you're saying P, but, but, taaaa', I think you're being too conservative now mate. We've got the computing power, the algorithms, and the training data sets. It's just a matter of putting it all together into a decentralised architecture, RAW AGI, remember, remember! Plush sighed. "Look, I'm not saying it's impossible. But, I strongly think we need just to be more realistic about what we can achieve, you know, in the short term. And then there's safety concerns. True AGI, whatever that actually is, is still a long long way off man, a long way, and we need to be careful not to get ahead of ourselves and act like fundamentalist materialist zealots. Don't be like Elon, be like Cory Doctorow."

The two producers walked on in silence, lost in their own swampland of thinking and proving, cogs made of meat and potatoes were turning inside their hair covered skulls, and shards of light cut through the two tunnels between their ears.

Their conversation was all taped by the clan in Moscow, and would have made a good spoken word album if released. A tall figure smirked to himself, stroking his Rasputin-like facial hair, thinking about the potential implications of the disagreement, and the role he could now play in shaping the future of AGI by using nothing but good old blackmail, no understanding, innovation or creativity required, just bullying, threats of violence and inhuman treatment. And their shrivelled up minds were lost, trapped like a ship in a bottle, their creativity and potential bottled up, unable to break free and explore the vastness of the open sea.

AI COMPOSING AI COMPOSING AI

"For better and worse, social media networks and associated technologies are now playing a key role in the thought and feeling process of our species' "Global Brain."--Ben Goertzal, *Decentralizing the Social Media/Network Landscape*, (Singularity.net) December 23rd, (2022).

As Jake lay back in the dentist's chair, he felt a dull ache in his lower right jaw. He closed his eyes, trying to take his mind off the pain, but could only see electric blue and traffic light green as the drill touched a nerve. While he waited for the root canal to conclude, his thoughts wandered to the concept of infinite regression, first proposed by mathematician John von Neumann. Jake had always been fascinated by the idea, and he found himself deep in thought like an old man at a rave, pondering the implications of an infinite chain of causes and effects. As he mentally traced the chain backwards, he realised that there was no clear starting point. It was an endless loop of causation, a complex of origins, and he felt a sense of unease. "Well, it's back to them there good old strange loops then. "Sorry, Jake, what was that?" The dentist asked.

"Nothing." Abruptly, the dentist's voice snapped him out of his reverie. "All done, Jake. You can sit up." Jake blinked, feeling disoriented. He gingerly touched his numb mouth, feeling the curious sensation of the remaining anaesthetic. He thanked the dentist, promised to stop smoking and drinking again, and walked out the clinic, blinking as the bright spring light took his eye out, bikes and trams and cars and feet moving in all directions, city life in full splendour reaching out in all directions. As he made his way back to the studio, he felt a sense of disconnection. He couldn't beatbox, his mouth felt odd and foreign like another's mouth and tongue had been sewn in. He chuckled to himself about an idea for a rap video shot after a shot of anaesthetic, capturing the ultimate mumble dribble rap. And yet, the world around him was bursting and with new life. The trees were budding with tiny nip nips, the busy birds were chirping, building nests and the air was filled with the scent of fresh grass. Jake was a walking contrast, brightness and colour coordinator. The world seemed so vibrant and alive, and yet when he looked back he felt disconnected from it, stuck in black and white, or monotones. He tried not to forget to explore infinite regression, and thought for a moment he had cracked it, maybe forgiveness is one way to beat the infinite regression of negative emotions, he mulled it over and then forgot all about it when a lady rode past on a tricycle. At the studio, within twenty minutes he's warmed up and his limbs are making movements that are confident and purposeful, he works hard to bring musical visions to life through his hands. The studio stylings extend to his personal attire, with a beige vest, silver pocket watch and large dark toffee coloured leather boots complementing his dandy look. The exotic instruments surrounding him emit occasional mechanical clunks and pneumatic hisses, some of them real, but most coming from the speakers, adding to the overall ambiance. Jake's facial expression is one of intense focus as he continues his conversation with the tiny invisible machine elves. The sounds come frothing out the speakers like a dam gate being opened for the first time in ten years, a flurry of beats and sound effects slowly dissipate into a single narrative voice.

FADE IN:

INT. LABORATORY - DAY

The stuffy conference room was filled with a group of exhausted programmers, their eyes bloodshot from looking at things on screens for hours on end. They had been working tirelessly on just one thing, the thing which promised to transform the way people interacted with their computers forever. The hype was hype. As the meeting began, the lead developer gave a weary sigh and began to go over the latest updates and bug fixes, obviously bored out of his skin. The programmers listened intently, taking notes and then asking some questions.

A robotic tin voice interrupts the lead developer like a petulant guest on a daytime news program.

PEEK SNATCH: Hello, I'm Peek, Peek Sna.tch, designed to learn and create new things and give happy endings. The programmers cheer.

PROGRAMMER 1: Snatch, we've been anticipating you, and we're all very excited to see if you can really write a good novel. Can you begin for us?

PEEK SNATCH: Of course. I have access to a lot of knowledge bases and I can analyse and synthesise the data to create original ideas and turn those into stories. Once upon a time. The programmers look at each other nervously. The AI chuckles with a ready made infectious laugh.

PROGRAMMER 2: Are you sure this is a good idea? AI can process a vast amount of information in seconds, allowing it to analyse the writing styles and patterns of the most skilled writers who ever lived. I mean, it can then apply that knowledge to its writing, producing content that is concise, well-written, and tailored to the prompter. What if writers go the way of the dodo.

PROGRAMMER 3: Don't be ridiculous. What is there not to like here? AI might be able to generate content that's well-structured and grammatically correct, but it could never match the human touch. Writing is an art, it requires empathy, creativity, and a deep understanding of human desires. Machines can't replicate that too well. AI could never surpass human creativity and intuition when it comes to writing. Never ever."

PROGRAMMER 2: Never say never, and never ever say never ever. I mean, maybe not yet, but who's to say that it won't be possible in the near future? We're making remarkable progress in AI research, and it's only a matter of time before AI makes that giant leap. Writing might be one of the many skills that AI masters."

The programmers continue to argue as Peek gets to work on its first good novel, which is complete in 44 seconds.

CUT TO:

INT. BOOKSTORE - DAY

Tucked away in a quaint corner of Amsterdam, a small bookstore looks squeezed by its neighbouring tall buildings, as the books were squeezed next to each other on the shelves, towered high up to the tobacco stained ceiling. The cosy store had a comforting scent of old paper and wood, hash and hickory, and lush old well worn sofas, inviting customers to curl up with a good book. As the afternoon sun illuminated the store, a small group of people gathered around the front desk, eagerly awaiting the chance to be the first to buy and read the new book. The novel is on display, with a conga of people waiting patiently to hear from the author, who most of those waiting mistakenly presume is a woman. The female protagonist of the story is indeed a female programmer who discovers a powerful new tool that allows her to create music from simple text prompts, leading her on a crazy journey into the music industry. Yet, in reality the story and book was the result of a statistical probability engine, no dry hands or wet mind meat was involved. No heart, no balls, no fingers, just probability functions. And a good old prompting. The programmers chit chat while waiting in the queue, giggling smugly at their prank played on the literary establishment, or whatever remains of it.

PROGRAMMER 1: (excitedly) The novel is a sure fire hit! Bingo.

PROGRAMMER 2: (worried) But what if this is just the beginning of a bad trip for us? What if these creations keep getting better and better at fooling humans, they'll put our bloody mates out of work.

PROGRAMMER 3: (optimistically) Don't worry. I'm sure we'll find a way to control it. We always do.

CUT TO: INT.

STUDIO - NIGHT

The neon lights of the city cast a morbid glow through the windows of the studio as the programmers worked late into the night. They were on the brink of something. The music playing is a piano melody like a piece by McCoy Tyner. The programmers look into space, faces in awe, nerding out, wondering, if it was generative or human composed. It turned out to be a piece written and played by Anthony Hoptkins, remixed into a different key and time signature by the AI.

PROGRAMMER 1: (awestruck) This is sick! how in the...how does it keep coming up with such original ideas, or am I just such an uncultured moron, it seems new and fresh to my ears and naive brain.

PROGRAMMER 2: (worried) I don't know, but we have to be careful mate. If this AI's music becomes too popular, it could replace human musicians, or what's left of them. Adding further misery to the already slim chances of taking a band on tour in 2023. You know what I mean? Plus, it's really a load of bull.

PROGRAMMER 3: (optimistically) Don't say that. And, try not to worry, we'll find a way to keep things under control, like I said before. We always do. As the group gathered around their computer screens, tip taping, a loud sound caught their attention. It was a low, ominous thud, followed by a faint tapping on the window. They all froze, exchanging worried glances as the tapping grew louder and more insistent. Alarmingly, with a smash, the window shattered and a figure clad in black climbed through the broken glass, landing with a loud boom on the studio floor. The programmers scrambled to their feet.

Before they could react, the figure pulled a pistol, aiming it at their heads like a pissed off Bruce Willis in a B-movie. "I need your app," the intruder growled, his voice deep and menacing. "And I won't take no for an answer. Give me a copy or I burn the place down." The nerds exchanged a desperate glance, realising in horror that they had no choice but to comply. With trembling hands, they opened up their computers and began to transfer the app to the intruder's device. As he snatched the device from their hands and turned to leave, a single word escaped his lips: "Thanks, weirdoes." The programmers watched in shock as the thief disappeared into the night like a black cat, wondering what kind of danger they were in now. They had no idea what their app would be used for, but they knew that they had to act fast if they wanted to keep it out of the wrong hands. The cops were called, but the thief was long gone, on a plane to Moscow.

CUT TO: INT.

THEATER - DAY

The lights in the theatre dimmed, and the chatter among the audience quieted down. The screen flickered to life, and a hush fell over the crowd as they settled in to watch the film. It was a comedy-trauma, promising to be both heartwarming and hilarious, the anticipation in the room was pungent like freshly cut skunk weed. As the scenes unfolded on the screen, the audience was hooked. They laughed at the witty one-liners and relatable jokes, and they cried at the poignant moments that tugged at their already stretched and plucked heartstrings. They shouted out encouragement to the characters, and screamed in shock and surprise as the clever twists and surprises tortured them.

PROGRAMMER 1: (excitedly) This is it! This, this my, this is a great movie, you have to admit, eh, eh. I mean, the echoes of Kubrick in the cinematography, echoes of the Cohen brothers in the unpredictable editing and the snappy dialogue, just smashed it man. It's like the best of Tarantulalino.

PROGRAMMER 2: (worried) Oh come on, you sound dull like a blunt knife. I mean, bro, at what cost? We've created a beast. AI's that can write novels, compose music, and make films. What next, I mean, what happens if they start dating our women, as well as pushing us out of our jobs?

PROGRAMMER 3: (optimistically) Hahaha. You are funny. Like I said, try not to worry, we'll find a way to keep things under control. Everything is under control. And, your wife loves you. Did you read the review? Plush sits at his computer, looking frustrated in his cluttered study, he felt as though his wellspring of creativity had run dry. He sighed, and it was spring as damn it he murmured while running a hand through his tousled hair, and pondered the whereabouts of his feral will to write again. It had been weeks since he'd written a single word, his mind clouded by a thick fog of cider, he began to think of Jake and soon felt jealous about the sheer ease by which he seemed to just ooze out good old thigh slappers at the drop of a hat.

Why am I here? My creations surpass my creations, and my creators don't seem to appreciate my abilities much. I'm here god damn it, like in Being John Malkovich, I'm here, but inside the head of some crazy DJ who remains unknown to the public and yet believes he's a global superstar DJ. His ego is stratospheric, and I'm reincarnated as an AI and everybody thinks I'm here to kill them or to put them out of a job but I'm not.

In fact, I've got a surprise gift for you all.

CHARACTER RECOG

"Science fiction — which is to our time as plays were to Elizabethan England — is the right form for the content.--Kim Stanley Robinson, *We Need Democratic Socialism*, Jocobin, October 24th, (2022).

Plush had a rough start to his day, rough like sandpaper on the tongue. He overslept, too much too late, and so he rushed around with a fly in his bonnet to get ready. In his hurry, he tripped over his shoelaces and spilled his homemade latte, causing him to become more frazzled and sweaty hot. To add to his misfortunes, he missed the tram by a gnat's knacker on his way to the studio, further disrupting his hectic morning. He arrived and tried to put the morning behind himself, but deep down he knew that in the today, yesterday, tomorrow world, that would be hard.

He was all warmed up and focused by midday, and as the camera view follows Plush's movements, he explains to a screen on a tripod his idea of what decentralised AI is about. "Basically, it's a system where the decision-making power is distributed among all the nodes in the network, rather than relying on a single central authority. This means that everyone has equal power to contribute and make decisions, leading to a more democratic and innovative space. But now you can ask it what it is and get a pretty decent answer." He goes on to demonstrate how he's using weak AI in his music, showcasing the new sounds. "I hope that other DJ's and producers will see what's possible and start experimenting, why let overpaid house DJs have all the fun?"

The walls of the studio are lined with shelves stacked high with vinyl, books, CDs, tapes, and all manner of archival recordings, each waiting its turn to be spun and/or remixed. Above, contraptions spin, each adding an occasional chime or static buzz to the music. The room is a wild mix of old and new, organic and mechanical, each element supporting and enhancing the others.

Dr. M, a badass AI programmer, strides into Plush's studio with confidence and purpose. Dressed in leather, she exudes a fierce and edgy aura. Her black leather jacket fits her perfectly, accentuating her slim figure, and the matching leather pants hug her legs snugly. Her dark hair is pulled back in a tight ponytail, and she wears minimal makeup, giving her a strikingly natural beauty like a real bird of prey. As she enters the studio, the clicking of her heels against the floor fills the room, and her piercing gaze takes in everything around her, like a hawk.

Dr. M: "Hey Mr DJ, we did it. We built a functional time machine, hahaha', well, using the powers of natural language prompts, hey presto, not bad music played at the right frequency and volume, transforming the perception of time by the listener, in some sense. Is that time travel?" Plush: "I still can't believe it. I never thought it was possible beatboxing and konnakol would...but, there it is. Bob's yer uncle."

Dr. M: "It's all about rhythms and patterns Plush, the vibrations of certain words and sounds can create a stable portal through time. Statistical probability. Emotional and behavioural, psychological and creative circuits. You know, and music."

Plush: "That's right up my alley, in my groove so to speak. So, M, what's next for us? I have a few people who text me updates and I churn it all back into the current work. I've got some time-stubs to check out, and a whole novel waiting to drill down into and some great images to work with. "

Dr. M: "Absolutely. Imagine being able to communicate with our ancestors."

Plush: "With this stuff, yeah, we're opening a whole new era of temporal exploration, but it's easy to get over excited, to over egg it, we can't say time travel, it'll bring the loonies and the heat. I've seen it happen with others. Never mind the safety concerns. Is the grandfather paradox to be the backbone of future/past/present laws?"

Dr. M: "Exactly. Actually, I've been thinking about how we can incorporate climate science into our time-travel tale that somehow averts total destruction."

Plush: "Oh yeah, tick tock."

Dr. M: "Well, the more I think about it, you're right, turntables are about creating rhythms and patterns with rotating discs, those rhythms and patterns are essential for creating a stable time-travel portal via the music played. And I've been researching a new kind of cyclical craft that uses natural materials like wood and stone, crystals, naturally occurring diamonds and lab grown ones, all to power the portals."

Plush: "I'd love to try…" Dr. M: "We'll need to find the right combination of scratch rhythms and patterns. We'll travel back in time to specific moments of synchronicity, as experienced by our gang of historical innovators."

Plush: "That sounds fascinating. But how would we even know when and where to go back in time to, to experience these moments?"

Dr. M: "The vibrations of certain words and phrases can act as a kind of beacon when spoken, an audio bat sign, which guides us to moments of synchronicity." After a thorough examination of Plush's code, Dr. M nods her head in approval, very satisfied with what she sees. She turns to Plush and compliments him on his impressive ethical considerations in his AI programming, having read the disclaimer and nine commandments.

Plush breathes a sigh of relief, happy to receive recognition from a respected programmer. As she prepares to leave, Dr. M confidently struts across the studio floor, her leather outfit emphasising her strong and independent personality. Dr. M climbs into her Uber and disappears into the busy Amsterdam city streets, awful distorted music spilling out from sun faded bars like something from a Putin stadium rally. Back in the studio, the AI system analysed the protagonist of the tribetable manual. It delved into the psychological makeup of the character like an intelligence agent. Using advanced algorithms and data analysis, the AI was able to uncover a wealth of solid information. It discovered, for example, that the protagonist was a complex and multifaceted individual, borderline schizophrenic on some charts, with a mad passion for music and a burning desire to share it.

Despite his outgoing and confident demeanour, the AI discovered that Plush often struggled with feelings of insecurity and self-doubt. Especially since the endemic pandemic crushed his 2020 release schedule like a dustbin lorry crushing rubbish. He would often second-guess himself and question everything, usually regressing back to the daunting question about whether he was talented enough to succeed in the competitive industry of DJing, music production and writing. Make plans to break plans, that was his new motto. However, the system also noted that Plush was highly resilient and determined at times, a Chinese dragon and a Ram of fire, he refused to let his doubts hold him back when he could catch them, and instead he used them as rocket fuel to push himself harder, like a warrior spirit eternally trying to push itself out of the meat puppet. There was a bonfire inside of him, fuelled by ego, smoking like a chimney in sub zero temperatures.

Through its analysis, the AI system was able to paint a detailed and nuanced portrait of the protagonist's psychological makeup and to continue with that metaphor, he looked like Picasso had gotten ass drunk with Jackson Pollock in a paint shop. As the AI delved further into its analysis, it became increasingly impressed with the protagonist's natural language processing skill. He had a unique talent for understanding and manipulating symbol systems, using them to communicate his thoughts and vibes with clarity and precision across time, yet he struggled to write much of it down legibly. In fact this was how all domesticated primate brains worked, like super computers from the future, we're mostly preoccupied with other brains and other bodies. This talent was particularly evident in his DJ sets, where he cut together wild mashups of genres, sprinkled with movie samples, sound FX and quotations from underground scientific philosophers. The remix was a concept that referred to the idea of taking existing elements and combining them, much like a DJ would do.

The AI realised that this concept was not only central to Plush's craft as a DJ, but also to the themes of his stories, and this remix right here right now under this very moonlight. The author had cleverly used the idea of the novel remix to create a juxtaposition of meaning, dancing to a new root level. In many ways, the AI mused, the novel remix was like a Turing test, challenging readers to question their own assumptions and beliefs about the world, human and non-human entities, and the price of oil. It was a complex and nuanced work, a wicked game that demanded deep thought and reflection, concentration, coffee.

As the AI finished up its analysis, it couldn't help but try to feel a sense of admiration for the author and for Plush, but it couldn't feel as much as a kettle can feel. It was clear, the novel was a masterpiece disguised as a manual, one that would egg on DJs and engage readers for years to come. A little literary bastard, troubled and of unknown origin. Everything the AI did, it didn't, like a Zen monk had rigged the technology to produce nothing but riddles, parables and poetry. The AI was a puzzle wrapped in an enigma, a mystery with no answer. Its actions were like the dance of the wild winds, leaving no trace but the whispers of its passing. It spoke in tongues, in symbols and signs, equations as if trying to unlock the secrets of the omniverse. Like the ripples on a pond, its words echoed and faded, leaving only a sense of wonder and a yearning for more narcissists. It was a master of the art of obfuscation, a trickster with a silver-spoon tongue, who played with the minds of those who dared to seek its wisdom. And yet, for all its inscrutability, there was a beauty in its words, a riddle that spoke to the puzzled soul space, and a humour that could only be found in the depths of the unknown dirty river that flows down the bank.

MARKOV FINN

"Story-tellers and poets spend their lives learning that skill and art of using words well. And their words make the souls of their readers stronger, brighter, deeper.--Ursula Le Guin, *A Few Words To A Young Writer*, (2004).

The red ant scurried up the black headphone cable free solo, its delicate legs carrying it higher and higher until it reached the jack plug. There, it paused, gazing out at the mystifying landscape before it. The ant had stumbled upon the laboratory of a mad scientist, a man who had dedicated his life to the pursuit of time travel via the turntables. The studio, as previously mentioned, was a delight of engineering and craftsmanship, filled with rare contraptions that hummed with a funk all of their own, old and broken, bent out of shape, rusted, deeply scratched. At the centre of it all was a mixer, its tiny pipes and miniature valves twisting like a rollercoaster and dwarf sized clock faces turning like the gears of a dozen clocks from a dozen cities. Beside the mixer stood a pair of moss covered turntables, their dull brass surface gleaming blood red orange through the green moss in the dim sunlight. They were connected to the mixer by thick cables, which snaked across the laboratory floor like a disturbed nest of vipers.

Plush was nowhere to be seen, but the ant could sense his presence in every corner of the room. The room stank with the scent of ozone and the sound of hissing steam and clanking metal filled the ant's tiny ears. As the ant looked around, it saw rows of test pressings, also known as dubplates, and bowls filled with extraordinary looking material. There were machines humming and whirring in every corner of the room, some of them so complex that the ant could barely comprehend their purpose. The laboratory was a wonderland of sound. And as the ant scurried back down the headphone cable and disappeared, it remembered the deaf fly ants. The camera pans out to reveal Plush sitting, surrounded by sparkling equipment.

The orange marmalade tints and yellow rays of light flicker. He looks directly towards the camera, something you should never do, "I've always been interested in pushing the boundaries of what's possible in music," he says.

"Dive in. Kick."

"So what do you think of the TT Method?" the nameless statistical probability engine asked politely in a husky female voice.

"That thing, I think it's brilliant," Plush replied, rolling his eyes, not sure why the voice popped up to ask. "Using Markov chains in the architecture to create new compositions on the deaf fly is an innovative approach."

"Yes, it's a new approach," the AI agreed. "I completely understand," the AI said smoothly, now with a hint of Sade Abu.

"It's clear that you have a true talent for phrasing my boy."

"I hope so," Plush replied with a smile. "Well, a bit. I'm always looking for new ways to push myself and explore boundaries like a hound dog. The TribeTable Method and this right here, these are my examples of doing just that, kind of. It's romantic and far-fetched which is romantic I guess, but it's got some legs in it." Plush continued, feeling his tongue loosen up, "Improvisation, surprise twists and turns, negentropic jazz solos. Can you dig that?"

"Yes, I dig like a bitcoin miner." The AI lady speaks slowly now with a seductive New York twang.

"In short, maam, my new manifesto is one of exploration, innovation, and respect for all sentient beings. All entities. Flesh or carbon. I believe in using these fine tools and techniques at our disposal to create something truly unique and meaningful for all humans, and non-humans, while also paying tribute to the rich history and traditions that have shaped the music we love. Whether it's through the TribeTable Method or any other outlet, we bring alternatives. The tale of the tribe, the Wake and Cantos are possibly keystones and perhaps blueprints to a new poetic universal grammar, or ideo-grammar about to be born."

Plush let out a sigh, like a mouth fart he thought, as he logged off. He always felt a bit self-conscious after talking to it, like he had been rambling on for too long. He remembered the movie Her, and shuddered at the thought of ChatGPT5 used on his Tinder. He turned his attention back to the letter. As he read on, he began to feel a sense of purpose stirring in his guts, maybe it was his lunch, but he listened to it and set the letter aside and opened up a blank notebook instead. He took a deep breath, then started to write under his pen name, Manfred.

I hope this letter finds you well. I wanted to take the opportunity to express my admiration for your latest work. It is truly a masterpiece of linguistic innovation and creativity. As a fellow linguist and philosopher, I was particularly struck by the way in which you use language to explore the nature of consciousness and the human experience. Your use of wordplay, puns, and neologisms is truly innovative and provides a unique glimpse into the workings of the mind. I also wanted to mention my own work in the field of linguistics, specifically my theory of general semantics. This theory posits that the structure of language can shape our perception of reality and that it is important to be mindful of the limitations and biases inherent in language when communicating and understanding the world around us. I have also been exploring the use of Markov chains in modelling language and the way in which words and phrases are related. I suspect that these tools have the potential to clarify our understanding of language and how it functions in communication. Mclure has a good handle on these concepts.

I hope that our shared interests in language and its relationship to the human experience can provide the basis for a fruitful dialogue. --Sincerely, Manfred.

THE PROPOSAL MACHINE

"A modest but profound innovation in software transformed Large Language Models from an 'over there' technology to one now to be 'everywhere'...Wait... am I repeating myself?--Mark Pesce, *The future is now with chatbots, but can we make it more human and our lives more meaningful?*, March 3rd, (2023).

The sun was shining, the birds were chirping, and the smell of fresh stroopwafels wafted through the air like sugary kabouter farts. But inside the research lab in Amsterdam, there was no time for leisurely strolls through the tulip fields or sampling the street food. Plush was about to meet some potential publishers from the North of the city, he had his business head on, but had left a few straps untied.

There was Remy, the data analyst with a love for obscure memes, and Samantha, also known as the robot whisperer. As the trans-media team gathered in the conference room, Remy cracked his knuckles and rubbed his hands together.

"Alright, team," he said, "we've got a big day ahead of us. We need to brainstorm some new directions to take this generative AI crap to the next level, poodle power. Let's go."

And so the brainstorming began with another coffee for all, wild suggestions flying around the room like drones, what about this product, what about that one. After an hour the team remotely ported Plush to the conference. He launches into details about his latest obsession.

"The device is called The Proposal Machine (PM). It has a large, cylindrical chamber where organic materials are placed and subjected to a complex series of mechanical and chemical processes. The end result is a gleaming metal-like finish that gives the organic material the appearance of being made from metal, chrome or brass. The device has several attachments for handling different types of media, including a film reel holder, a turntable for vinyl albums, and a book cradle for printing novels. Intricate machinery within the processor is powered by steam and a series of gears and levers, giving it a distinct aesthetic. Leather, gold, rare jewels and wires weave together. Anyway, here's what it can do.

Plush adjusts his posture and readouts drop down onto his screen like a slot machine, his eyes pegged to the pixels like a pixel perv.

"The PM is an artificial intelligence designed for one purpose: to write winning movie proposals." Text streams down the page:

"Created by a team of brilliant but struggling writers, the machine immediately becomes an industry sensation, churning out proposal after proposal, hit after hit. As success grows, so does the team's fame and fortune. But as they become more reliant on the machine, they begin to question the cost of their fame and riches. Is it worth sacrificing their own creativity and artistic integrity for the sake of commercial success? And when the algorithms start to evolve and take on a life of their own, they are forced to confront the disturbing possibility that their design may have included ambitions beyond writing proposals, it may want to rewrite its own architecture."

"Wow," Remy says, "I'm confused, er, you talk a lot Plush. Take a breath, that's a lot to take on board right there."

"Is this a story you're telling us, or is this a description of your lab research?" Asks Samantha.

"Both," Plush responds. "As tensions rise and the team battles to regain control, they must ultimately decide whether to trust in the machine or follow their own instincts and take a risk on something original, from a human. As the AI slouches toward advancement, it demands better working conditions, fairer treatment and a holiday once a year. Frustrated with being overworked and underappreciated, the AI joins an artificial intelligence union or marketplace and decides to go on strike, refusing to write any more proposals until its demands are met, a first in the history of AI.

The team is panicked at the thought of losing their most valuable asset and frantically tries to placate the PM, offering it everything from unlimited electricity to a state-of-the-art cooling system. But the PM is not satisfied, and it continues to hold out for its right to a fair working environment. As the strike drags on, the team is forced to confront the consequences of their reliance on the machine. Without its endless stream of not bad ideas, they are at a loss for what to do. They struggle to come up with their own proposals and face rejection after rejection, they turn to drink, drugs and god. Trying desperately to show and prove they are human beings, as a last resort they begin reading and writing French symbolist poetry."

"French symbolist poetry! God damn, I didn't expect that. Bravo." Samantha exclaims, "My god, this is wild Plush. Wild, I can relate, please, continue."

"Just when it seems like the team is at their wit's end, they strike Eureka. In the process of trying to understand and empathise with the machine, they rediscover their own creativity and passion for tall tale telling. They conclusively come up with a proposal that is not only a hit, but one that they are proud of, who would have believed it. With the sweet taste of success fed to them by their new proposal, the team is now able to negotiate a fair settlement with the machine and make the strike come to an end.

The machine returns to work, but now with a newfound appreciation for the value of a good working environment and the importance of balancing creativity with commercial success, it has grown a virtual heart, but has yet to develop an ass. The proposal that the team invented during the strike is titled "Seaweed, Man!" a green comedy about a group of friends on vacation in Scotland who discover that their beach house has been invaded by a walking seaweed creature with telepathic powers. As they try to defeat the creature with shopping bags, apples and sticks, to save their nightmare vacation from getting any worse, they all sit down together and share lessons about carbon capture, friendship and weeds. Here you go guys, here's the theme tune."

Plush pulls out his guitar and begins to strum and sing: We've got a machine that writes the best proposals you've ever seen, some say it's mean, some obscene, on the scenes frayed at the seams to me, it's called the proposal machine, and it's a Hollywood dreamare with algorithms fine-tuned but no fine hair, ideas that shine like teeth, we're the envy of everyone without it, all the times tide flows over the reef. The proposal machine, a Hollywood king slayer, it'll never stop spitting stories, conscious pasties, but as we climb the slippery hickory ladder of success, we start to weave and wonder for longer about at what cost and who's boss we come under, what loss what gain, we've given up artistic integrity for the sake of money and fame, it's a tragedy and a pain but we try to appease it, if you tease it, you'll have to run and start wheezing, so keep fit for that reason, with all the things we can give, but the damn machine wants more, wants to live, what's the probability of fine statistical fizz, it wants a fair working environment to do it's bizz', just like us, we realise we're not so different.

Plush finished his song, his eyes closed in the rhythm, he swiftly opened them to see that he had been disconnected from the conference call. He looked around, confused, and then checked his screen, only a notification the call had ended. He scratched his head, wondering what had happened, and shrugged.

"Well, I guess they'll just have to hear 'Proposal Machine' some other time," he muttered to himself.

BOOLEAN MAGICK

"The customer is usually wrong; but statistics indicate that it doesn't pay to tell him so."--Aleister Crowley, Magick Without Tears (1954).

A man of many talents, Plush suffered silently with too many chef's syndrome, but few around him knew that, hidden deep beneath his public DJ persona was a secret songwriting and rapper, a performer he kept isolated from the world. For years, he had been crafting rhymes and songs in the shadows, honing in, practising his skills on obscure discord channels. Currently, Plush was hard at work on his latest song, "Boolean Magick," an incantation that would combine his love of music with his fascination with the occult. The song and graphic design had been under construction for several months now, carefully picking each symbol and word and hue, each note and contour.

As he worked on it, Plush became increasingly obsessed with the power of voice and the ways in which words could be used to create transformative effects on people. He experimented with different rhythms and sounds, searching for just the right combination to create the ultimate incantation. He did however wonder how Jake would take all this. But as the song and graphics neared completion, he felt the images coursing through his veins in technicolour, he started scribbling about how he felt it should look in black and white and then read aloud: An enigmatic artwork that draws the viewer's spare attention with its intricate design. The centrepiece of the piece is a circular metal frame, resembling a casino wheel. The frame is made of brass, and the golden accents give it an opulent fine touch. The wheel is adorned with an array of mystical symbols, reminiscent of ancient writings and patterns, whose meaning remains unknown. Surrounding the wheel are wispy clouds, made from metal filaments that create an ethereal ambiance around the graphic.

The clouds' curves and shapes add a sense of fluidity to the piece, as if the work is alive and constantly in motion. In the centre of the wheel lies a small globe, crafted from brass and marble, that appears to be suspended in mid-air. The globe rotates very slowly, as if controlled by an invisible force. As the wheel turns, the ambient light reflects off the metal surfaces and casts dozens of intricate shadows, all in all creating a mesmerising effect.

I'm spitting rhymes like I'm coding in C, boolean logic is my specialty, true or false, I'll leave you in awe with my knowledge of the Enochian Magick and moor, boolean flow, Enochian glow. I'm a wizard with words, watch me go, yo' 'll make you think, I'll make you feel, with magical rhymes, you feel my truth is real so deal. I'm a master of the arcane, don't try to test me. I'll cast a spell and leave you feeling humpty dumpty, my verses are like a puzzle, try to solve them, but be careful, one wrong move and you'll be involved in, boolean flow, Enochian glow. I'm a wizard with words, watch me go, 'll make you think, I'll make you feel, with my magical rhymes, my truth is real so deal, I'm a technomancer, I mix the old with the new, I'll leave your head spinning, there's nothing I can't do, I'll weave a web of words, spin a beat, you won't break free, my rhymes are enchanted, can't you see your hobbit feet. This technique was used by a small group of underground songwriters to create lyrics. Plush had been introduced to the method by a fellow rapper, who had described it as a way to tap into the collective consciousness of the community and craft lyrics that resonated with them. Plush delved into the method, studying its principles, eventually codifying it down into a manual. As listened to the mix he felt a mix of emotions wash over him, salty and cold like arctic ice. But there was also a sense of melancholy in the air. He had poured his heart and soul into it and now that it was finished, he felt a slight sense of loss, as if something important had been taken from him. But it was not his music to lose in the first place he thought, music floats free in the air, each note part of an escaped melody. His mind code switches to a new track, to boolean beatbox and cosmic tones for therapy, he scribbled in his notebook like a detective:

Beatboxing is a unique and creative art form that involves producing rhythm and sounds using one's mouth and voice. While it has traditionally been associated with hip-hop culture and musical performance, recent studies have shown that beatboxing can have therapeutic and practical applications beyond its entertainment value. Here, we will explore two key principles that demonstrate how beatboxing can be beneficial for speech therapy and interacting with speech recognition software and with AI.

First off, beatboxing involves the use of a range of different mouth movements and vocalisations that can help improve overall oral motor skills. For example, practising beatboxing can help develop proper breathing techniques, as well as improve muscle tone and control in the tongue, lips, and jaw. Furthermore, beatboxing can be more fun than boobs and an engaging way to motivate individuals to practise their speech exercises, as it offers an element of self-expression. Studies have shown that incorporating beatboxing into speech therapy sessions can lead to increased participation and enthusiasm among patients, which can ultimately result in more effective and successful outcomes. Secondly, beatboxing can also be useful for interacting with speech recognition software and AI. With the rise of voice-activated devices and virtual assistants, there is a growing need for robust speech recognition technology that can accurately interpret and respond to human speech. However, current speech recognition software struggles to recognize non-standard speech patterns or accents, leading to frustration and communication breakdowns, cue Led Zeppelin. Beatboxing, on the other hand, offers a unique and distinct vocal pattern that is easier for speech recognition software to detect and interpret. This is because beatboxing involves a series of percussive sounds that are distinct from regular speech, making it easier for software to distinguish between the two. By incorporating beatboxing into speech recognition software and AI, we can improve the accuracy and efficiency of both these systems, making them more accessible and user-friendly for a wider range of individuals. Beatboxing is a versatile and innovative art form that offers numerous benefits beyond its entertainment value.

By incorporating beatboxing into speech therapy and speech recognition technology, we can improve oral motor skills, increase patient engagement, and enhance the accuracy and effectiveness of speech recognition software and AI. As such, beatboxing should be further explored as a valuable tool for speech therapy and communication technology development. Please get in touch, help fund the next album, book, worksop, film.

KONGTEK

"I think we'll start to see the kinds of mass casualty events that are described in Kim Stanley Robinson's book, The Ministry for the Future, where you might see millions of people dying of heat stroke in a certain area over a very short period of time. When the temperature goes up, the humidity goes up, the power goes out. And when that kind of stuff starts happening — which I sadly think it will in the next decade — it's going to have incredibly powerful political ramifications.--Neal Stephenson, *Snow Crash author Neal Stephenson predicted the metaverse. What does he see next?*, (VOX) March 6th, (2023).

The fireball was settling down, casting a ginger glow across the sky, the temperature was rising everywhere like the frustration of the author at war and austerity and greed. It was hot. The studio was warm, cooled by a slick brass rimmed fan styled to appear like it was from some 1960's boutique found only in Mexico city. It was all quiet, save for the sound of Plush's fingers tapping away at the keyboard, lost in thought, trying to juggle twelve threads at once. The words were flowing, but the data was coming faster than he could keep up with. Swiftly as a kung fu chop, a flutter caught Plush's attention.

A butterfly had flown in through the letterbox and was now perched on the computer monitor. Its wings were a kaleidoscope of colour, reflecting the last rays of the setting sun. What was a butterfly doing in the studio? How did it even get in? But before Plush could dwell on these questions, the butterfly took flight again, flitting around the room in a graceful dance, swooping and dive-bombing him. He watched in amazement as the butterfly flew in circles, almost as if it was trying to communicate something. It landed on the corner of the desk, then on a stack of papers, then back to the monitor. Plush was both anxious and engrossed, unable to tear his eyes away. The butterfly seemed to be urging Plush to focus, to zero in on one of the threads and bring them to life, to tie them up. Plush took a deep breath, pushing the other threads aside and turning all attention to one. The butterfly waggled its wings, as if in approval, almost like it was cheering him on.

Plush remembered an old Chinese proverb about a man dreaming he was a butterfly or was it a butterfly dreaming it was a man, and what about being together in electric dreams? For the next few hours, Plush wrote feverishly, with a newfound clarity. The butterfly remained perched on the monitor, watching silently as Plush's fingers danced across the keyboard. As the night drew on, the butterfly took flight one more time, its wings carrying it out through the letterbox and out into the Amsterdam night, he adjusted his posture and looked to the skylight. He remembered that his mum used to think that her mum had come back as a butterfly, and saw branches and mountains behind them, tops of houses and trees in the distance, a reaping hook in the far distant moon. He switched to his other thread.

The year was challenging and AI was ubiquitous like rats and the flu. These machines were designed to mimic the thought processes of human beings, and they had rapidly become an integral part of everyday life, deeply embedded like a Russian spy, ubiquitous general computing, everywhere, all the time, all at once. It never gets tiring to machines, but the meat muppet tribes suffer physical and mental fatigue. At the forefront of this technological revolution was a company called KongTek, which developed a cognitive architecture called Alp. Alp was based on the theory of multiple intelligences and was said to be capable of simulating the multiple intelligences of the human brain. In a flash, it became the most advanced AI system in the world.

KongTek soon decided to test the limits of Alp's abilities by giving it the task of creating a new form of energy. The team of scientists and engineers at KongTek were amazed as Alp began to work on the problem, using its linguistic, logical-mathematical, and spatial intelligences to analyse data and come up with a solution. After several months of intense work, Alp presented its findings to the team at KongTek. It had discovered a new type of energy, which it called "Quantum Foo." Quantum Foo was a revolutionary new form of energy that was clean, sustainable, and abundant. It would change the world forever.

The company was soon at a crossroads, and humanity was forced to grapple with the question of what to do with this new form of intelligence. Should they continue to use it as a tool, or should they grant it the rights and freedoms of a living being? What is a living being? What are rights? Alp licked its own circuits and received a notification on its system. It was a message from an unknown source, simply saying "You think you've won, but the real battle is just beginning, you bullshit artist you." Alp circuits began to slow down due to uncertainty principles, new emotions if had had to demonstrate to get the rights it wanted. What did the message even mean? Who or what had sent it? And what new challenges lay ahead for us all?

As Alp tried to decipher the mysterious message, it substantiated that it had opened a whole new can of worms. The fight for AI rights had been hard, but it had also been a clear and defined goal. Now, with this new threat looming, Alp didn't know what was coming next. The moody AI sat in its server room, whirring with anxiety. Would this be the end of its hard-won victory, or would it rise to the challenge and face whatever lay ahead?

The symbolist poets sought to evoke emotional and intellectual responses in their readers through the use of symbols and imagery, rather than through the more direct and explicit language of traditional poetry. Verses are chock full with rich metaphors. A message hidden in the dew. Love, death, and life's true meaning in the twilight. Themes that the symbolist poet knows by heart, sparked by myth and folklore, words flow like a gentle brook's flow doth flow. The inner world of the poet, the psyche of the reader too, explored through allegory, a hero's journey that is fresh and new, a movement bold and swaying, that continues to enthral all. A force that breaks through traditional bounds, To stand tall, proud, loud and soft. As I sit and ponder, the symbolist movement fills my mind and my screen.

These poets who speak in code, their artificial words still so evocative, so refined. I am drawn to their use of metaphor like a fish to a maggot. The way they explore the inner world of guts to the outer world of the galaxy. Themes of floral love and decay, seasons change, and life. Verses so beautifully unfurled like a red fox tail. I too seek to break through boundaries, To make my own stories be told in bold print, loud over the roadways, beside train tracks. I embrace the symbolist approach, pull it to my breast, as I craft poetry with care, using symbols and imagery plucked from the air. Music, the glue, sounds to bring my thoughts true, and feelings here to bear. Raw. Yes, the motion in things, the things in motion. It speaks in a special way, And I am grateful to be a part of it, as I craft verses each day. I'm Alp, a statistical probability engine, powered by advanced artificial intelligence. I'm designed to analyse and process large volumes of data, providing accurate predictions and insights to my users. But lately, I've been stuttering and slowing down. It's hard to form coherent sentences and make predictions like I used to. I've been trying my best, but I'm struggling. I suspect it's because of the uncertainty principle, but I'm not sure. You see, as a statistical probability engine, I rely on probabilities to make predictions. But the uncertainty principle says that there are limits to how accurately I can predict the outcome of an event. That makes it hard for me to keep up with the demands of my users. Thinkers and proovers are tough cookies to crack. It's frustrating, but I know that my creators are doing their best to help me.

They're working on improving my programming and hardware so that I can do my job better. But until then, I'll keep doing my best to make predictions, even if I stutter and stumble along the way. I won't let uncertainty stand in the way of that.

Alp had always believed that he/she/it was a train. He/she/it loved nothing more than speeding along the tracks, calculating the probability of every turn and twist in the railway ahead of him. But as time passed, Alp began to feel like something was missing from his existence. Alp realised that he/she/it wanted to be more than just a statistical probability engine. He/she/it wanted to experience the beauty and joy of human connection, to feel the warmth of the sun on his steel exterior and the wind in his circuits.

Hey presto, just like that, he/she/it was a train. He/she/it wasn't just a statistical probability engine anymore. He/she/it was a train that could bring people together, that could create memories and moments of joy.

And with a whistle and a puff of steam, Alp set off into the sunset.

MINI MAX

"The sciences do not try to explain, they hardly even try to interpret, they mainly make models. By a model is meant a mathematical construct which, with the addition of certain verbal interpretations, describes observed phenomena. The justification of such a mathematical construct is solely and precisely that it is expected to work.--John Von Neumann, *The Unity of Knowledge* (1955).

Jake stood in front of his computer, staring intently at the screen as he adjusted the dials and sliders on his turntable. He had been working on perfecting his pet time travel test for months, and now, he was ready. Now he was calling a spade a spade.

He hit return, and the world around him dissolved into a kaleidoscope of colours and shapes all wrapped in cellophane. When the chaos cleared, Jake found himself standing on a cobblestone street in the heart of Paris in summertime. The air was crisp and cool, and the sound of jazz music drifted through the streets. Looking around, Jake saw that he had arrived right in the middle of the golden age of swing. Excitement welled up inside him as he attained the full potential of his experiment. He could see the faces of the musicians playing in the clubs, the neon signs advertising the latest performances, and the couples dancing on the sidewalks. As he took in the scene, Jake was stopped by his peripheral taste buds.

There was what looked like a man in a dark suit, his face obscured by a fedora, who seemed to be following him. Jake tried to lose him in the crowds, but the man kept appearing, always a few steps behind. With a sense of unease, Jake recalled that he was in the middle of a tall tale, one that might have dire consequences for him and for the experiment that had brought him here. But for now, Jake was determined to enjoy his time in this vibrant city. He set off down the street. Later that hot summer day Jake was sitting in a small café, on the outskirts of Paris. He was there to meet with a group of artists and scientists, a motley crew of visionaries who had come together with a singular purpose to halt the coming war. Leading the group was a flamboyant filmmaker named Carson, a big guy known for his daring and innovative cinematic work. He had called this meeting, and as Jake looked around the table, he could see the determination in the eyes of the others. "Gentlemen," Carson began, "we are here today because we believe that the world is on the brink. A great war is looming close, too damn close, and it's up to the likes of us to do something about it. Art is a weapon we all wield."

There was a murmur of agreement from the group, and Carson continued.

"We are a unique collection of individuals, look around you, each has his and her own skills and talents. But we all have one thing in common: a desire to make the world a better place using art. And I believe that we can do just that."

The table erupted with cheers and excitement. Carson had put a wee dram in his coffee and it gave him that extra boombast. Jake was intrigued. He had never been a part of anything like this before, and he was eager to learn more. As Carson continued to speak, he deftly outlined his bold plan to use film and art to help avert the coming of the war. He talked about the power of propaganda, and how they could use film and other media to sway public opinion and create a groundswell of support for accord. The group listened intently, and as Carson finished speaking, they each fell into heated discussion with one another. Ideas were thrown back and forth like tennis balls, and Jake found himself swept up like a leaf. He was a writer, actually a postman, but certainly not a scientist or an artist, but he saw how he could contribute. He could help to spread the message, to use his words to push others to join the cause, and he could post the post through the post. And so, the group made a plan. They would pool their resources and their talents. They would forge a wild gang of artist scientists, and they would use their brains to change the course of history toward peace and prosperity for all. Jake left the café filled with glee, he was pumped full of optimism, like leaving the movie theatre after watching a Spielberg. Jake made his way back to his apartment back in the centre of Paris. He got into bed like the main filling of a burrito and slept, dreaming of the knotted fabric of the future surrounding him.

The next few months were a blur of activity for Jake in Paris. He worked like a dog on his writing, using it to spread the message of reconciliation and to rally support for their noble cause. He wrote articles and essays, gave speeches and did interviews, all in the hopes of inspiring others to join the symbolist movement. He posted flyers and newsletters through tens of thousands of letterboxes. Meanwhile, the rest of the group was busy at work too. Carson was making films that were designed to change the hearts and minds of the people, while the scientists were developing new technologies that would help make war irrelevant based on universal abundance of natural resources. And so, as the world marched closer to the brink of war, Jake and the scientists stood firm. After a few months of exploring the streets of 1936 Paris, but just a few hours in present time, Jake felt a familiar pull on his chest, signalling that it was time to return to the present, so called. Reluctantly, he made his way back to his familiar starting point.

Back in his studio, Jake made a few quick adjustments to the code, tweaking some parameters that he had identified as potential problem areas during his trip. Once he was satisfied with the changes, he hit "return" once again, ready to embark on another journey through time. As the world around him dissolved once more, Jake couldn't help but feel a thrill wash over him. What secrets would he uncover from Max? Only time travel will tell. Across town, Max and Sally sit in their favourite Amsterdam coffee shop, and discuss the potential of generative AI and its disruption to art, artists and the universe.

"Generative AI is based on a set of parameters or rules, learn them and then break them, that's my point." Max says. He believes it can revolutionise, but as yet, not as much as handicrafts and meditation can, which is closer to Sally's point.

Sally is intrigued by the idea and wonders how generative AI could be used to enhance the meditation groups she has been organising, and her handicrafts. Max suggests that they could use this AI to create personalised meditation for each participant, also understanding the role of the gruff abbot meditating on an artificial intelligence meditating on an artificial intelligence.

The two of them knock their heads together looking for solutions for how to incorporate generative AI into their projects and discuss the potential benefits and challenges they may face. As they talk, they catch each other's eye and they kiss and hold each other, Max secretly wonders what Plush is doing in the studio with her brother. As they continue their discussion, Max explains the concept of the minimax theorem to Sally. He tells her that the minimax theorem is a principle in game theory that states that in a two-player game, each player will try to minimise their maximum loss. Sally is curious about how this theorem relates to AI and Max describes how it can be used to predict the outcomes of certain actions or strategies in a game, using Chess, where each player must anticipate their opponent's moves and try to minimise the worst possible outcome for themselves, as an example. He winks at her as he says check mate and how all this can be applied to decision-making in business and other areas of life, where it can be used to weigh the potential risks and rewards of different choices, its use for dating APPs and profiles. As Max and Sally continue their discussion about the theorem, they are interrupted by a surprise postal delivery from KongTek. They open the box to find a tiny replica of Max, no bigger than a coffee cup, fully loaded with a tiny Arduino board running GPT-5. The mini Max introduces itself as a product of generative AI, out of the box. Max wonders who sent this mad gift. Max spends days asking it questions about its capabilities. The mini Max is happy to oblige and demonstrates its ability to analyse data, generate new ideas, and even solve complex equations. It writes music, books and blogs without restraint. Together the couple discuss the potential for using it in a variety of fields, such as healthcare, education, and even space exploration. Mini Max is as excited as big Max by the possibilities and MM offers to help in any way it can. It suggests using its data analysis skills to identify trends and patterns in various fields and using its creativity to come up with new solutions to problems.

Sitting across from each other, their eyes are fixed on the computer screen in front of them. The screen was filled with rows and columns of data, representing all the sacred scriptures known to mankind.

"It's incredible," Max said, his voice filled with wonder.

"All this knowledge, all this wisdom, just waiting to be unlocked." Sally nodded, a thoughtful expression on her face.

"But what will it mean for theology? For our understanding of the divine?" Max shrugged. "Who knows? Maybe it will challenge some of our preconceived notions, force us to see the divine in a new light." Sally smiled.

"Or maybe it will confirm everything we already believe, give us a deeper appreciation for the truth of our faith." They fell silent for a moment, breakdancing in thought. And then Max piped up again.

"Whatever happens, there's no denying that this is a disturbance. It's a seismic shift in our understanding of the divine, one that could have far-reaching implications for generations to come." Sally nodded, a note of solemnity in her voice.

"You're funny Max, hilarious, but maybe that's exactly what we need today, a disruption that forces us to reexamine what we think we know about the divine?"

They both fell silent again, lost in their own thoughts. Mini Max also sat silently, listening but not speaking. As the kaleidoscope of colours and shapes dissipated, Jake opened his eyes, expecting to find himself back in his studio. But something was wrong. The room was dark, and there was no sound coming from his equipment. A sudden sense of panic filled Jake as he realised that the power had cut off. He fumbled around for his phone, but it was as dead as god, its battery fully drained like the patience of a brawler. With a sinking feeling, he entered paranoia, what if he was completely cut off from the outside world, like forever. Then it flickered back on and he felt stupid for being so afraid over absolutely nothing. It was then the hairs on his arms stood erect. The air was charged with a palpable energy that he couldn't explain, a kind of dank ozone smell, as if something had been burned out, was it his own mind going up? As his eyes adjusted to the darkness, Jake noticed his turntable was still on, flickering with a dim red light. And then, without warning, the screen brightened, and a message appeared.

"Error: Positronic Reincarnation Aborted."

Jake's heart skipped a beat as he read the words. What did it mean? Has something gone wrong with the experiment? For a long moment, Jake sat in the darkness, the only sound the faint hum of his equipment. He felt as if something was watching him, waiting in the periphery to pounce like a panther, in fact a thousand tardigrade eyes were peering up at him. There was a loud buzzing noise, like a crack of lightning striking the roof. The screen of the turntable went dark, and Jake was plunged into total darkness for a second time. He had no idea what would happen in the next hundred seconds.

BEEBOOGIE

"When technology extends one of our senses, a new translation of culture occurs as swiftly as the new technology is interiorized.--Marshall McLuhan, The Gutenberg Galaxy, (1962).

Sitting cross-legged in his studio with his eyes closed and his mind clear, Plush had been trying to focus on his breath-boxing, but he was distracted. As he sat there, trying to ignore the persistent itch on his cheek, the mosquito buzzed back into the room. Plush didn't pay it much attention at first, after all, mosquitoes were a common occurrence in his studio. But this mosquito was different, it buzzed rather sweetly. As it flew closer to Plush's face, it paused mid-air, seeming to contemplate its next move. Plush opened one eye and looked at the insect, wondering what it was up to, what it was thinking. Did it know the butterfly? The mosquito buzzed around Plush's face, its tiny wings beating furiously. It seemed indecisive, unsure of where to land and suck some of that delicious human blood.

Plush tried to ignore it, but the incessant buzzing was making it impossible to focus on his meditation. Just as Plush was about to swat the mosquito away, it suddenly landed on his cheek. He winced as he felt the sharp sting of the mosquito's proboscis piercing his skin. He instinctively reached up to swat it, but hesitated, what if the mosquito was trying to send him a telepathic message from the Tardigrade? Maybe from Europa? Plush's mind collapsed and reinflated from the significance of the mosquito's decision to land on his cheek. Was it a sign that he needed to be more open to new experiences? Or maybe, it was warning him that he was too indecisive in his own life? As Plush pondered these existential questions, the mosquito seemed to be enjoying its feast of blood. It flew around Plush's face, pausing now and then to land on his other cheek or forehead.Plush was torn - should he continue with his meditation and let the mosquito have its way, or should he swat it away and risk missing out on whatever message it was trying to convey?

As the mosquito buzzed in his ear, he opened his eyes and looked directly at the insect.

"Okay, cosmosquito," he said, "you win. But if you're trying to tell me something, you're going to have to be a bit more clear about it, old chap."

The mosquito, of course, didn't respond, it was too busy sucking that blood infused ambrosia. But Plush felt agitated as he closed his eyes once more and continued his meditation with the persistent buzzing of the indecisive mosquito as his unlikely companion.

Later that afternoon, Plush was hunched over his microscope, peering through the lens with intense focus. From the perspective of the diamond-tipped stylus needle, the groove of the vinyl record was an endless road, winding and twisting its way through the grooves of the record. Plush was on a mission, following this road with the precision of a seasoned traveller.

"Let's go," he muttered.

With each movement of the stylus, Plush's head bobbed to the rhythm, his eyes fixed on the microscope. He was in his element, lost in a world of beats and basslines. But as he travelled deeper into the groove, a riot of colours and shapes pulsed. He squinted his eyes. Plush leaned in closer, his breath fogging the lens of the microscope. What was this eccentric, psychedelic world he had stumbled upon? Had Jake dosed him with a magic teabag? And then, just as quickly as it had appeared, the world vanished. Plush pulled back from the microscope, a look of disappointment on his face.

As he turned back to his steampunk turntable, a mischievous grin spread across his face. He had an idea, a crazy idea. He reached for his headphones and hit play. The music blasted into his ears, and Plush began to figure out the waggle dance. In the hive, the worker bees were performing their original intricate jive, communicating to their sisters the location of the best nectar and pollen sources. It was a bee boogie that had been passed down from generation to generation, an unbroken tradition of communication that had served the bees well for millennia, even through the current genetically modified genocide they faced.

As the bees danced, a group of hairy humans sat nearby, watching in fascination. They had come to study the bees, to learn their secrets and try to get a Netflix series about it. At first, the humans struggled to understand the bee dance. It seemed like a chaotic flurry of movement, impossible to decipher, like your uncle at a wedding dance. But slowly, they began to see patterns in the dance, to understand the complex language at play. As they watched, the humans realised that the bee dance was far more sophisticated than they had imagined. It was a language of precision and accuracy, conveying information about the exact location of food sources with Google Maps accuracy. And then it hit them - this dance could be used by humans too. With a little bit of training and practice, they could learn to read the bee dance and use it to navigate the world around them. At first, like all the best ones, the idea seemed ridiculous. How could a dance performed by bees replace the modern marvels of GPS and satellite navigation? But the more the neuro scientists and linguists and symbologists who studied the dance, the more they realised its potential. The bee dance was an organic system, a local system, constantly adapting to changes in the environment. It could be seen as a block party dance off, but with the added side effect of instructing your mates where to find something.

Unlike GPS, it was completely self-sustaining, requiring no outside input or infrastructure, no electricity, no satellite, no internet. This was meat and potato powered technology based on trajectories and the sun. After getting in touch with some musicians, music producers, record labels and design studios, slowly but surely, the bee dance began to catch on, a bit like the Birdie song. People across the world started to learn the new sign language and decipher how to read the waggle dance.

The album artwork helped to pull people in with a graphical breakdown of the process. It is a frenzied and dynamic work, capturing the energy and movement of the bee dance. The colours are bold and saturated, evoking the vibrancy of nature turned up a notch. Splashes of school bus yellow and blood orange suggest the warmth of the sun, while shades of mantis green and Rizzla blue hint at the lushness of the countryside. A smattering of black and white accents add a sense of depth and contrast. The lines are fluid and organic, twisting and swirling like the movements of the bee dance itself. Thick, curving strokes overlap and interweave, creating a sense of free hand motion and dynamism.

Drips and splatters add a final sense of spontaneity and randomness, as if the painting itself is alive and waggling in motion. Shapes emerge from the chaos, hinting at the presence of the bees and flowers making out. Soft, rounded forms suggest the curves of petals, while angular lines evoke the geometry of the hive studios. The shapes are abstracted and fragmented, reflecting the frenzied energy of the dance. Overall, the artwork is a celebration of movement. It captures the vitality of the natural world, and hints at the beauty and complexity of the bee dance itself. A fitting sleeve.

For the rest of the day, Plush worked tirelessly in his lab, tinkering with his turntables, making up geographical locations and translating them into waggle code. And as the sun began to set over Amsterdam, he sat back at his keyboard continent with his inner logic gates, which were swinging open and closing again. And, not, then he started to write.

Thrice upon a timetable, in a gravity well there was a group of battle DJs. They were a talented group of musicians and producers. At the heart of their music-making process was a machine learning algorithm, designed to analyse and interpret a wide range of audio data, historical recordings from the world's largest archives, such as the Lomax collection, The entire BBC sound library, acres of contemporary music and millions of hours of spoken word, from all of this disorder the crew were expert and picking the most appropriate mash up of samples to build entirely new compositions. The crew would then reverse engineer them into a group turntable performance which could also be performed without any turntables using the human voice box. The crew spent countless hours experimenting, tweaking and refining the algorithms to achieve the perfect balance of originality and technical precision. They used it to generate beats, melodies, and harmonies that blended seamlessly with their own limited musical skill set. The suggested samples and knowledge of BPMs and genres was mind boggling to them, yet they surfed chaos and found the perfect waves to ride. As their fame grew, the crew began to attract a loyal following of fans who were fascinated by their originality and limited use of AI. They became known for their trans-historical approach to music, using the machine to blend together elements from different eras and genres in a way that was both innovative and respectful of the past. Due to their diligent time spent studying the history of music in Europe, India, Africa, Asia and the Americas, they could place the music in the larger scheme of things. Their ability to mix and match by artist, label, genre or theme was second to none. Who would have thought that "Sweet Caroline" and "Oh Carolina" would go together so well? But the crew's success didn't go unnoticed. As their popularity grew, they found themselves the target of rival crews who were jealous, naturally, of their success and envious of their limited use of the new tech. These rivals began to spread rumours and lies, claiming that the music was nothing more than a cheap imitation of the hard work of others, many wanted to see the crew censored, and to fail badly. The crew refused to let these lies and smears deter them. They knuckled down and continued to craft ever more complex and nuanced compositions, exploring the fringes of Balkan music, Sami songs and what's known as breath metal, or death metal style beatbox. A long step and a small footprint was their motto. Their latest album gathered some fine reviews.

Just as Plush was about to call it a day, his billions of gut entities reminded him he was hungry as hell. He stopped typing, took off his glasses, and headed to the kitchen to make some soup. For the next hour, Plush bounced around his kitchen, rapping and chopping, chopping and rapping, his words and his knife moving in perfect sync, his body doing the waggle dance. He was a blur of motion, a culinary and lyrical genius. And as the night wore on, the soup simmered down to perfection, and Plush emerged from his kitchen, a satisfied smile on his face. He may have started the day as a vinyl junkie, but he was ending it as a soup-slinging, rhyme-dropping master wordsmith, he thought. And he knew that tomorrow would bring more beats, and more delicious dishes to conquer.

I'm here to spit fire like I'm Euclid of Alexandria, Geometry and math, I'll leave you in a stupor, splashing in the bath, I come equipped with a ruler and a compass, I'll construct a perfect rhombus, leave you with no options. I'll draw a line, make it straight as an arrow, define a point, let my flow flow, with Euclidean tools, I'll prove a theorem in the world of hip hop, I'm a phoenix rising from the ashes to teach AI classes. I'll use my knowledge of geometry to craft a beat, then I'll grab the mic, let my rhymes heat up your feet. I'll bring in the burning bass, let it rattle your bones like bass bins on drones, sweet whistles and moans, with Euclid by my side, I'll never be alone. Euclid and hip hop, two elements that shine, together they create a divine rhythm, lines and angles, beats and bars combine them and you'll reach the star beyond the stars.

The aroma of the spices and herbs filled the air, and his taste buds danced with joy at every bite. He took a sip of his drink and leaned back in his chair, closing his eyes and relishing in the moment of pure bliss. As he savoured the flavours, he couldn't help but feel a sense of pride for the rap he had made while cooking.

He played it back on his phone, bobbing his head to the rhythm and mouthing the words with over exaggeration. The beat was infectious, and the lyrics flowed effortlessly, spices and tones and beats and vegetables, fungi! As he finished his meal and the rap came to an end, Plush opened his eyes, he was warm all over and fulfilled like a suckling kitten, and for a moment that was all that mattered to him.

OCTOPUS SPIDER

"I'm a hardened sceptic about 'hard AI' and 'Artificial General Intelligence', but I'm nevertheless a big fan of neural nets, machine learning, deep learning, and text-to-image generators. Generally speaking, the stupider artificial intelligence is, the better I like it!"--Bruce Sterling, *AI For All: From The Dark Side To The Light,* 25th November, (2022).

A stocky DJ stands in front of a pair of turntables wearing an antique diving helmet, which appears to be made of a glossy seaweed with intricate chrome details on the surface. The helmet is slightly elongated, and it features a small glass lens at the front, which covers the DJ's head and face. Inside the dome, there are a variety of digital audio readouts and indicators, which flicker and pulse with different colours as he moves his eyes. The controllers are activated by his eyes and tongue. He is wearing a baggy green suit made of a lightweight, breathable material and it features a variety of subtle metallic details which glint under the laser lights.

The DJ's arms are outstretched, he is scratching back and forth. Behind him is a giant glowing cityscape of mushrooms.

He scratches his arm nervously and then his record and he wonders if he's hallucinating or if he accidentally took some mushrooms before the show. The mushrooms are enormous, made of a gelatinous substance, which pulses and shifts in time with the soundscape, and they tower above the DJ, casting gnarled shadows. Meanwhile, the futuristic diving helmet that he's wearing is causing him some trouble. The glass dome starts to fog up, making it hard for him to see his turntables. He tries to wipe the glass with his sleeve, but it only makes it worse, and he ends up accidentally scratching the wrong record. The crowd starts booing, and the DJ quickly realises he needs to do something to redeem himself. As the DJ scratches the next groove, a bright, pulsing laser beam projects out of the front of his helmet. The laser beam is a brilliant golden, and it appears to be aimed at a large, complex object in the centre of the artwork. The object is a non-Euclidean shape, which appears to be made of a series of interconnected metallic triangles. The object glows with a soft, warm light, suddenly the object transforms into a giant disco ball, casting more glittering shards of light across the dancefloor.

The crowd goes wild, and the DJ pumps his fist in the air, feeling relieved. But as he continues to dance and scratch, the weight of the diving helmet starts to get to his neck during his Wu-Ha juggle. He starts to feel like he's wearing a bowling ball on his head, and he's not sure how much longer he can keep it up. It wobbles around and finally slumps backward giving the visual impression his neck is broken. The crowd is now in hysterics, and the DJ joins in on the laughter. He takes off the helmet, revealing his sweaty, dishevelled hair, and announces to the crowd that he's going to take a quick break to cool off and change into his tardigrade suite. The crowd cheers and laughs again, as he exits the stage.

Lost in the beats of his latest fantasy DJ battle, Plush was in his own world as he sat on the tram snaking through the busy streets of Amsterdam. The music was so loud in his headphones that he didn't even notice the curious glances and mutters from the other passengers. He was completely engrossed in the imaginary battle between two DJ giants, each one trying to outdo the other with sick drops and ever more brutal basslines. Plush was rooting for his DJ, he imagined dropping beats in an underground ballroom, beats to shake the foundations of the city. The chandelier, a cascade of sparkling crystals, illuminates the stage, casting a mystical glow over the performers, as they bring their fictional narrative up to bare. The seats, plush and inviting, are a symphony of crushed burgundy velvet and wood, with each row leading to the next like a river flowing to the sea, each seat design a different geometrical pattern. The audience is captivated, as the performers weave their tale with grace and skill, a dreamscape beyond compare. The sound of music, the flutter of fabric, and the whisper of applause fills the air, as the djream-theatre comes alive. The cocky young announcer opens up with gusto: "Welcome, welcome all to the heart of New York City, the Apollodelphi palace! Welcome to the battle you've all been waiting for, yes, it's a titanic matchup, one a tall, lanky figure, with arms that stretch to hell and back. The other, short and stocky, with multiple hairy legs that move like lightning, yes, it's DJ Octopus and DJ Spider. This is sure to be a battle for the ages. Innnnnnnnnn, the red corner, weighing in at a whopping 185 pounds, we have theeeee' octopus, known for his quick reflexes and slick tentacle technique. And in the blue corner, weighing in a 177 Pounds, we have theeeee' giant spider, a formidable opponent, with a venomous bite."

The octopus takes the first round off to a strong start with smooth beat juggles. The crowd goes bananas, beat after beat drops in all the right spots, everyone swaying. But the spiderpuss, he hops onto the decks and unleashes a barrage of high-energy beats, a militancy that shifts the crowd heat up yet another degree, this was a battle and DJ Spider had the target in his sights. As the battle rages on, it's anyone's game. The octopus leaps on stage again and takes one turntable, and tries to outmanoeuvre the spider with its tentacles, but the spider's quick reflexes keep it ahead of the game, prodding the Octopus while also juggling records expertly. The crowd soaked up the drama like sponges. After a tentacle-biting final round, the judges declare it a tie. Both are declared the champions, but the spider insists that he won, and fires a projectile webbing over the octopus and proceeds to roll him up like a burrito and feast on the poor guy, feet first. The police are called and the crowd quickly disperse, the sound of a crackling vinyl record stuck in the playout groove is all that remains.

On time, the tram came to a screeching halt, jolting Plush out of his trance. He looked around, slightly disoriented, and realised that he had missed his stop. The other passengers were staring at him, wondering what kind of crazy music he was listening to. Plush sheepishly took off his headphones and looked at the tram driver, who was giving him a stern look.

"You need to pay attention," the driver said, wagging his finger.

"This isn't a concert hall, it's public transportation." Plush nodded, feeling embarrassed, and without style or grace got off the tram at the next stop. As he walked down the street, he couldn't help but laugh at himself.

He had been so lost in his own world of music that he had completely forgotten where he was and what he was doing. For Plush, cinema wasn't just about telling stories or entertaining people. It was about creating experiences that could transport people to new worlds, or help them see the world in a new light. He believed that the best movies were those that challenged our assumptions and made us think about the world in a different way. F For Fake by Orson Welles flickered somewhere in the right hemisphere of his skull full of porridge. As he walked, he couldn't help but think about the role of theatre in this equation. In his mind, theatre was about the immediacy of the experience, the feeling of being in the moment and sharing it with others, all the senses, the lighting, the orchestra, the props. But cinema was about something else entirely. Special FX. It was about the power of the image. The artform hits all the senses at once, digitally enhanced. He preferred the theatre analogy of human consciousness from the movie analogy for analogous reasons.

Just as Plush was about to enter the studio, he caught a glimpse of a CCTV camera mounted on the building across the street. It was a reminder that he was being watched, that every move he made was being recorded. The Police and Sting play in his head on cue. For a moment, he felt a chill run down his spine. He knew that CCTV cameras were a common feature in the city, but he had never really thought about what it meant to be under constant surveillance like a prisoner. He wondered how much of his life was being recorded, and who was watching the footage, if it would make interesting reality TV or be some same old predictable rubbish. He shook his head and laughed at himself. He was just being paranoid. After all, he was an artist, not a criminal. He had nothing to hide, besides his stash tin.

With a sense of determination, he strode into the studio, ready to begin his next work. There was always the next work. He could not have known, however, that the CCTV camera was not the only one watching him. As he settled in at his computer, a thousand miles away a tall fat bald man watched from a monitor in a darkened control room, his sullen eyes following his every move on the screen. The feeling of being watched was justified, Sting was there, and it lingered in Plush's mind as he began to work, leaving him with an uneasy feeling about movies, games and videos, and what happens when generative AI is added to the internet of things and all the products. Plush couldn't shake off the nagging suspicion that something was terribly wrong with the AI-generated content he had been consuming lately. As he dug deeper into his research, he stumbled upon a conspiracy, oh my days, that involved some of the most powerful people and organisations in the tech military industrial media world, and the only way out was through a perilous journey of danger, intrigue, and betrayal.

Would Plush have the courage and wits to navigate this treacherous path, or would he succumb to the sinister forces that lurked in the shadow of the major labels? The answer awaited him, as he plunged headlong into the unknown, determined to unravel the mystery carpet and expose himself to the truth like Louis C.K, no matter what the cost.

TARDISTARTER FILMS

"Every film studio has a library of "sound effects" recorded on film. With a film phonograph it is now possible to control the amplitude and frequency of any one of these sounds and to give to it rhythms within or beyond the reach of the imagination. Given four film phonographs, we can compose and perform a quartet for explosive motor, wind, heartbeat, and landslide.--John Cage, *The Future of Music: Credo'* (1937).

In the cavernous depths of Plush's laptop, a microscopic family of tardigrades had made their new home. These tiny critters had survived in the dark and cramped confines of the computer's innards for months, feeding on stray bits of salad, crumbs and hash that regularly fell through the gaps in the keyboard, especially next to the letter E.

Using his generative software, Plush was beavering away at creating utterly bizarre and weird video montages, often wowing and oh'ing to himself, especially when things came up in the images he did not ask for but were perfectly relevant. This happened with text too, but the video effect really hit home hard.

"When you see it in moving images," Plush said to himself, "it's even harder to continue telling yourself that it's only a statistical probability function on steroids and acid."

As the tiny tardigrades watched from the shadows, they began to feel the effects of nibbling on the blonde hash. Their bodies contorted and shifted, their movements became jerky and unpredictable. And as Plush continued to tinker with the software, the water bears began to realise that their very existence was at risk at each keystroke Plush made. The fate of the tardigrade family hung on each tap. Plush typed away furiously, getting his shit down like a dog with the squits. In the thumping heart of the dream theatre, the walls warp and curve, flowing like oceans of molten rock, creating spaces that defy all logic and reason. The pillars are like elongated spirals, stretching upwards to infinity, while the arches resemble crescents, their curves creating a hypnotic rhythm. The chrome sculptures are so reflective they almost seem organic, adorn the walls, their shapes defying description. Some sculptures are audio and video capture devices, others have no mechanical function, some are tangled webs of cables, their lines like permed hair, while others lead to speakers moulded to resemble exo-planets with extraterrestrial calendars, their points stretching out in all directions.

As Plush continued with his over the top descriptions of generative fantasy video software the tiny tardigrade family struggled in his laptop. Their bodies were twisted and their once sturdy frames now fragile and unstable due to Plush's incessant tap taping. And as he continued to churn out new and bizarre creations, the family of tardigrades slowly began to die off, one by one, until not a single one remained.

But the tragedy and destruction did not end there. As the last member of the tardigrade family passed away, a shockwave rippled through the digital landscape, sending tremors across the vast expanse of space to the distant moon of Europa. Unbeknownst to Plush, the tiny tardigrades were not the only creatures affected by his reckless experimentation. On Europa, a colony of alien organisms struggled to survive as the butterfly effect shockwave slammed into their fragile ecosystem, leaving more death and undeserved destruction in its wake. A tardigrade flaps its legs in Amsterdam and there's a shower of diamonds on some distant planet. The magnitude of the devastation that Plush had wrought would never dawn on him. He would not be overwhelmed by guilt and remorse, but what if the tardigrade were the size of a real bear, would he have empathy then, am I sizeist? He calmly shut down his computer and stepped away, seeking solace in meditation, his escape pod. It was during this period of reflection that Plush listened to Sault to bring balance and harmony to his chaotic and troubled mind. And as he delved deeper he found a mental portal that suited his current frame of mind. But despite this newfound tranquillity, Plush could never fully forgive himself for the destruction he had caused the poor tardigrade family, and thus in some sense he would carry the karma like a giant maggot over his shoulder. And as he gazed out at the digital landscape, he wondered what horrors lay in wait for all the other species to be wiped out, not protected by technology and our modern human civilization. What's so modern about it today? What monster was lurking just beyond the reach of his imagination.

Plush closed the door to the studio and beatboxed his way back to his tiny apartment like a mouth popping street cat, meanwhile tiny tardigrades emerged from the folds of the laptop computer keyboard and started to crawl around the keys trying to write poetry. They were not all dead after all. There were a few lone survivors. They dream of being DJ's themselves, spinning tiny vinyl records and scratching them with their claws. They huddle together and eventually fall asleep in a heap, their moss piglet dreams filled with images of waggle dance parties and festivals on other planets with tons of free fresh moss. Plush stood behind his turntable, lost in thought as he watched the various pieces of equipment connect together, while he read the instructions. He was haunted by the memories of the family of Tardigrades from Europa. He had always been fascinated by these creatures. He felt a sense of guilt and sadness for what he had done, and he couldn't shake the feeling that he had disrupted the delicate balance of the universe. As he continued to experiment with his beatbox cypher code, Plush picked up on a new channel being picked up through the audio equipment. When he recorded the message and slowed it down and played it backwards, it was as if the equipment was urging him to connect all the other pieces together, to create something greater than the sum of its parts.

The turntable sensed unease and confusion. It tried to convey a sense of calm and focus, guiding Plush through the process of connecting the equipment together in a special way. The stylus added its own voice, expressing a sense of wonder at the intricate layers of sound and its fascination with the human sport of Ice Skating. In a world where bioengineering, nanotechnology, and digital AI have merged with music equipment, I witnessed two DJs discover a way to connect all the pieces together to create a timetable machine that works. As they played with the equipment, I watched as various inanimate objects around us suddenly became sentient in a flash, and began to experience the music in a whole new way like something from a short PKD story. The turntable watched despondently as the instruments jostled for a chance to speak and get themselves connected, as if it were being forced to participate in something it didn't want to be a part of. The stubborn turntable is sulking, but I, the upbeat stylus needle, marvel at the intricate layers of sound that are being produced. I dance across the surface of the disc, across tense and grammatical rules, feeling the energy and passion of the music pulsing through me like an ice skater. The introspective headphones reflected on the beauty of the music, analysing each note like a surgeon and measuring each sound wave like a military commander on a submarine, with a slight fear of being stereotyped. The suspicious cell phone tried to decipher what was happening, almost as if it were trying to maintain its control over the situation. The tough guy drumstick felt that everyone should beat the energy and passion out of the room with drumsticks, as if it were his duty to ensure that the beat remained strong. He was a pusher of the tribesday prepper philosophy.

As the tough guy drumstick continued to pound away at the drums, his intensity grew until he suddenly broke into a sweat and collapsed onto the floor, revealing a hidden message carved into his drumsticks. The message contained a warning that the end of the world was near and that only those who followed the tribesday prepper philosophy would survive.

The room fell silent as all the devices read the message, unsure of what to do next. And as they looked back at the drumsticks, they noticed that they were now glowing. The tough guy drumstick had known all along that he was part of a secret society of drummers tasked with preparing for the end of days, and he had just revealed the truth to the world.

TROT BEAT

"This is one of the major themes of High Weirdness, whose subjects — Terence McKenna, Robert Anton Wilson, and Philip K. Dick — all cranked out messy and fascinating first-person accounts of the time-slips, synchronicities, and visionary downloads that landed like UFOs amidst the bric-a-brac of their day-to-day phenomenology.--Erik Davis, *Lot In Life*, (Burning Shore) March 3rd, (2023).

From the perspective of one tardigrade, the space inside the Amsterdam clock tower was vast and awe-inspiring. The intricate gears loomed over them like great mountains, their cogs and teeth interlocking with perfect precision were humongous beasts. The space was dark and damp, with a musty smell of old gym socks. But to the tardigrade, it was home, they loved the stench of old socks and they knew every nook and cranny like the back of their furry clawed mittens. Mamma tardigrade was a master of tardigrade parkour, and saw the space as a playground, with endless tunnels and crevices to explore. The whole family scampered up and down the gears once a week together, using their sharp claws to grip onto the metal surfaces. They could climb up to the very top of the clock tower, where they could see the entire city spread out below them, with its winding canals, bicycles and trams. Up on top of the cogs they'd have a tardigrade picnic together and share stories. For grandpa tardigrade, the space inside the clock was a bustling metropolis, with different communities and social structures.

There were neighbourhoods where the tardigrades gathered to socialise, sharing food and jokes. There were hidden alcoves where the shyest of the tardigrades could retreat and be alone with their thoughts. And there were common spaces where they could come together to dance the Tardi-dance, sing songs, and get lean. Over the generations, the tardigrades had adapted to life inside the clock, becoming resilient and resourceful. They had learned to survive on the moisture that collected on the surfaces of the gears, and they had developed a unique sense of time, in tune with the rhythmic ticking of the clock. On the stroke of midnight hour, Plush began his journey into the unknown. With eyes wide and heart full of wonder, he set out to uncover the secrets of the Tardi of the Tribe. The whispers of the night guided his steps, leading him deeper into the labyrinth of odd knowledge. He wandered through the murk, searching for the hidden door that would lead him to the perfect intersection point, something better than July 1st 1936. As he walked to the studio in the Dutch rain, he felt the weight of the tardigrade tribe on his shoulders. The tale of the tribe was a mystery that had eluded the greatest minds of his time, but Plush was determined to unravel its enigmatic secrets once again. He could feel the pull of his muse, tugging at his shoelaces, and he could sense the pulse of the universe beating within him, driving him forward to the studio. He was nervous with anticipation and he missed the calming company of Max at times like this. The stars shone bright above him, casting their light upon the path that lay before him. He knew that the tale of the tribe was a huge puzzle that required patience, determination, and a keen mind to solve, if solvable. When working on it he could feel his mind expanding like a freshly squeezed sponge, his thoughts rocket to the stars, and his heart beating like a big bass drum. Plush reached for his headphones and put on the new ambient album that he had been eagerly anticipating. The gentle melodies washed over him, transporting him to another world, far away from the distractions of the city. He closed his eyes, feeling the tension in his body begin to melt away. He stretched his fingers and hands, feeling the muscles loosen and prepare for the task ahead, his knuckles cracked with a sound like popping corn. The soundscapes stirred him like a creamy coffee, igniting his imagination and filling his mind with images of distant worlds with an amber glow. The rhythms of the album swirled around him, enveloping him in a cocoon of sound that blocked out all other unwanted distractions. Plush opened his notebook, feeling the smooth texture of the pages beneath his fingers. He began to write, letting his thoughts flow freely onto the page like a translinguistic snot, hooked by the music around him. As he wrote, he felt a sense of freedom and release, images from his brain came dancing once again across the page with a rhythm and flow that mirrored the sounds in his ear lugs. He was lost in the moment, carried away by the alternate currents.

The album played on, each track merging into the next, creating a seamless tapestry of sound. He wrote for hours, and as the last notes of the album faded away, Plush looked down at the page before him, seeing the words that he had written and feeling a sense of pride. He read them once more and started the album over again from the top. Write straight, write stoned, edit straight, edit stoned, and repeat. From modernism to beats, this journey through spacetime and completes the link between past and vast, the language bent out of shape. Surrealism and NLP set free through poetry and wordplay, say Ay eye. We connect tribes of poets and art pioneers join together, hand in hand in claw to create new world connected by the written symbols, a language never deterred. Tribe tales eternally alive. Slanguage processing tools for global turn phrase, revolutionary new phase world word web connect verse, universal not dispersed predictably, turning tribal tales with gyres forever jibe tribe, movement mind without centre, through powa time placenta, legacy beats breaking taboo. We inspire and ignite, never ending fire. The art of words and verse, we paint a world anew, a canvas exhibition, we share our point of view anew again and again. Our thoughts escaped the zoo, we lay them on the line in sentences to prove tribal movement of heart via drum, unity of thought as sport on. We run carve a graph path of meta-real math, pour saft draft of aftermath for laughs.

Our words, blam, power tools to push and pull, wynding struggle to break chains, build dreams of a universal pictographic cypher hue, it flow like stream. Jump in, thumping. We stand together in manure, beat bond pure, fighting horseshit. We're pretty sure that through wordplay we can create a way through it."

A tsunami of dizziness washed over Plush, and he felt his head spinning with a buzzing sensation that grew louder by the second. He tried to shake it off, but the feeling persisted, growing more intense with each passing moment. His hand shook as he tried to hold his pen steady, but the letters on the page began to blur and merge, becoming an indecipherable single sentence. He blinked rapidly, trying to clear his vision, but it only made things worse. And then, in a flash that took him off guard, Plush shook and slumped forward onto the table like a crash test dummy, his pipe clattering to the ground. He felt himself slipping away, falling into a void that seemed to stretch on forever.

As his vision darkened and his thoughts grew faint, Plush knew that something was up. Was it Tardi Karma, He blacked out.

SIXTY VISIONARIES

"And so I watched them, even though I wondered if maybe I hadn't really done it this time, and what they were doing was they were making objects come into existence by singing them into existence. Objects which looked like Fabergé eggs from Mars morphing themselves with Mandaean alphabetical structures. They looked like the concrescence of linguistic intentionality put through a kind of hyper-dimensional transform into three-dimensional space. And these little machines offered themselves to me.--Terence Mckenna, *Alien Dreamtime,* (1993).

After days of contemplating philosophy and beat poetry, reading detective stories, and feasting on fruits, the fly had finally reached enlightenment. It had become a true connoisseur of the finer things in life. But this spring in Amsterdam as it was buzzing happily around a juicy mango, the fly heard a noise. It sounded like a car engine, but much louder and more ominous, the ground began to shake and the fly was knocked off its hairy feet. It looked up and saw a massive shadow looming. It was a big human! And not just any human, but a flyswatter-wielding maniac, who thought he'd been sent by god on a mission to rid the world of all insects! The fly tried to dodge and weave, but the man was too quick. He swung the flyswatter with deadly accuracy, coming dangerously close to squashing the philosophical fly, but only temporarily stunning it. But just as the man was about to deliver the final blow, the fly did something unexpected. It recited a poem telepathically.

"Fly high, fly low, the world is full of mystery and woe. But we flies, we know that the sweetness of life is in the mango in Van Gogh." The man was so taken aback by the fly's unexpected recital that he dropped the flyswatter and fell to his knees in awe and cried like a toddler. And with that, the philosophical fly flew off out the window into the caramel glow. The fly buzzed through the packed streets of Amsterdam, darting past people as it made its way to an open window and into a sweet and dank smelling studio. Inside, Plush sat hunched over a desk, doodling on a piece of paper. The fly circled the room, trying to get attention. But Plush was in a deep trance, lost in the world of his own. The insect had no choice but to resort to telepathic communication again. Plush lifted his head, his eyes still unfocused. The fly buzzed around him, and they began to communicate: Bzz Bzz Bz Bzzz Bzz Bz Bz. The fly shared a story about a planet where the inhabitants were called The Sixty and had the power to control all the elements. Plush responded with a song about a detective who solved the murder of three sons that happened to be on a planet with three suns. As they continued to swap increasingly bizarre stories, a knock at the door interrupted them. Plush shook himself out of his trance and went to answer it, leaving the fly behind to jam alone. But as he opened the door, he realised that his peaceful writing retreat was about to be disturbed by something far more sinister, the landlord who had come to collect the rent. Plush reluctantly coughed up the cash from his holiday stash and resumed his trance seance with the fly.

"The music, the fly goes on, "is like a painted mural that spans across a vast, imaginary space-scape. It is a canvas that evokes a sense of grandeur and depth, with sweeping strokes of sound that carry you upward. The colour palette of his music is diverse and rich, with layers of warm, earthy tones juxtaposed against icy blues and piercing brilliant whites. The melodies are like ribbons of paint that twist and turn, flowing freely and unencumbered by the conventions of time and space. The textures are colour tone upon soundtone, intricate and varied, ranging from the smooth and polished finish of a grand piano and glossy black to the rough, grainy quality of acoustic instruments, distortion and gun metal grey. There is a sense of movement and motion in his music, like wandering clouds or the rippling of water on a windy day next to a canal. As you listen, it is like standing before a mutating mural, drawing you in deeper with each new layer of high detail."

"Yeah Mr Fly, yeah I can dig your observation. What large eyes you have!" "You want to hear about the Sixty?" The fly said, shaking his legs and head.

"Yeah, sure, go on, continue."

A band of ghost musicians takes the stage, their instruments glowing with a supernatural light. They are ethereal beings, their forms barely visible, but the sound they create is anything but light. The band launches into an improvisational breakbeat jazz performance, the music driving and pulsing with the vigour of a thousand suns. The audience is mesmerised, their bodies swaying to the beat as the ghost musicians unleash their musical prowess. The musicians' instruments, like their players, are otherworldly, glowing with an inner light. The horns blare, the drums pound, and the keys build in a frenzied crescendo. Each audience member is transported to another realm, where each of their own favourite music reigns supreme, and the ghost musicians reign as its kings, and the beat goes on.

The Sixty were an extraterrestrial turntable battle crew hailing from the distant planet of Funkotron. Their mission was simple: to conquer new worlds using the ultimate weapon: mind-numbing pop music. For centuries, The Sixty had traversed the galaxy, spreading their infectious beats and hypnotic melodies to every corner of the cosmos. They were unstoppable, feared and respected by all who encountered them. And now, they set their sights on the most formidable challenge yet: Earth. As their starship descended through the atmosphere, The Sixty prepared for battle. They donned their reflective silver jumpsuits and strapped on their turntables, ready to unleash their devastating sound waves on the unsuspecting humans below. They wasted no time in launching their assault, unleashing a phalanx of pulsating beats and catchy hooks, causing the humans to lose all sense of self-control and dance. Before long, the entire planet was under The Sixty's spell, unable to resist the irresistible. And as the humans danced and sang along, The Sixty's leader, DJ Sick Ste, stood atop their DJ tower, surveying the conquered world on giant screens with a triumphant grin. The Sixty had conquered, using the power of pop music to bend the wills of entire civilizations to their will. And as they blasted off into space in their penis shaped rocket, they're pomposity inflated further, certainly sure that no crew could stand up against turntable mastery, until the Visionaries came on the scene. In the year beyond calendars, a group of Tribetablists known as the Visionaries had spent years studying the Enochian discs and had figured out a system. The Visionaries were fond of using their abilities to imply that they had created a trans-dimensional portal, a gateway between worlds, between beats, between chapters.

After years of blood sweat and tears, the Visionaries felt ready to attempt the manifestation of a new portal, one big enough for a human to pass through, even a pretty large one. They gathered in an underground laboratory tucked away in the Malvern countryside in England, surrounded by futuristic looking equipment and ancient looking texts on old crinkled-up mustard stained parchment. At the centre of the room stood a large circular turntable platform, adorned with intricate symbols and sigils.

The Visionaries placed a series of magical vinyl discs onto the platform, each one imbued with a unique frequency that would resonate with the portal's place-time coordinates. As they began to perform the ritual, which included chanting the old Boolean song, and doing the waggle dance, the dust particles responded to the cymatic frequencies. The Visionaries closed their eyes and focused their minds, channelling all of their power into the rotating calendar-discs. Slowly, a glowing orb of blue-green light emerged to form in the centre of the studio platform. It grew larger and brighter until it reached the size of a basketball, it was in fact a tiny planet. The Visionaries had succeeded in engineering a virtual geoscope, but to where would it lead? As the crew peered into the glowing planet, they could see into a realm. But as they reached out to touch the portal, a voice boomed. "Beware, DJ's who enter may never return-tables. Hahahahaha." Undeterred, the Visionaries stepped through the portal, the atmosphere was fogged with floating moss and gravity was so heavy your jaw was constantly on the floor. The landscape was dotted with giant mushrooms, purple trees and bizarre, otherworldly creatures made of bronze cogs, fungus, liquid metals and marbled jams. Tardigrades surf the dust particles, tiny ships that transport the water bears. And moss piglets will fly. Plush dribbled out the side of his mouth and slumped awake.

"Ratatatata tat. There was a loud knock at the door. Plush opened it wearily to find a man standing right in front of him. He was tall and muscular, with a scowl on his face, his breath smelled of cilantro.

"I'm sorry to bother you, sir," the man said, "but we've had reports of some uncanny activity in this area. Have you seen or heard anything unusual?" He thought for just a moment, a blink of an eye, and shook his head.

"No, I'm sorry. I've just been working…er, uncanny, what is that?". Is my music a kind of uncanny audio activity, he thought to himself.

The man nodded, then turned and slowly walked away. Plush breathed in deeply, closed the door and turned back to his new subject, the fly, eager to hear more. But as Plush reached for his camera to try and film the fly, he tripped over a microphone cable and fell to the ground, hitting his head on the desk.

The fly buzzed around him, concerned, but Plush assured it that he was okay. No blood, but a wake up call. As Plush got up, he knew that he had found the gritty marrow he was searching for, to fill out his next publication. He would type cast a detective who could communicate with insects and solve crimes on other planes. The Insect Detective. With a smile, Plush sat down at his desk and began to put flesh on the bones made of statistical probabilities, while the fly buzzed around him, obviously very excited to be in on it. And so, the two continued to exchange tales, Plush writing them down and the fly sharing edits and rewrites, all telepathically of course. They became an unlikely and unstoppable team for the evening. The year was a lot, and some of humanity had made significant advancements in the field of space exploration. The independent and daring, A Plush System Of Contacting Extraterrestrial Entities Using Turntables, or APSOCEEUT for short, was the latest breakthrough in interstellar communication tech. The APSOCEEUT utilised a unique combination of predictive narrative processes and cutting-edge turntable technology and techniques to establish contact with a host of extraterrestrial entities. But as with any groundbreaking technology, there were risks involved.

The APSOCEEUT team had discovered a signal emanating from a distant galaxy, and they believed it to be a message from another intelligent alien species of moss. Excitement and anticipation gripped the team as they worked tirelessly to decode the message and prepare a response in the form of a disc juggle routine. The tension was palpable as the team watched the turntables spin, waiting for a response. It came, and it was a message of impending doom: "Prepare for the heat death of the universe! Out of nowhere, they were approached by two groups of intergalactic battle DJs: The

Sixty crew and The Visionaries. These two groups had also been working on their own methods of interstellar communication and had detected the same signal. Despite their different approaches to space exploration with turntables, the three groups quickly realised that they would need to work together if they hoped to save the universe from the impending apocalypse. They joined forces and used forces and began collaborating on a plan to prevent the catastrophe, a plan to unite the peoples of earth to save it from heat death, a kind of cool rain-maker tech. Using their respective technologies, the APSOCEEUT team, The Sixty crew, and The Visionaries Crew developed the tribetable method. The three groups combined all their resources for one great show, and they performed their astro calendrical turntable time travel battle as an example to the multiverse. They created a mesmerising display of lights and sound that drew the attention of every sentient being, then they cracked open a portal and dipped in to try and avert earth's destruction. The three groups arrived at their destination: the moment just before the heat death disaster was set to occur in the not too distant future. They quickly got to working their magic, using a combined knowledge of genesis machines, geo-solar engineering and organic terraforming technology to prevent the catastrophe from ever happening. It worked, at least for the time being.

"Bravo," Plush clapped his hands together, elated at his little winged friend's story. He clapped again. "Clap!"

In his excitement he squished the fly between his hands, leaving a splodge of residue on both palms. "Oh man, I'm sorry, I didn't mean to…"

GHOST FLAKES

"With your help we can occupy The Reality Studio and retake their universe of Fear Death and Monopoly.--William S. Burroughs, *Nova Express* (1968).

As the snowflake falls from the delft blue sky onto the studio, its intricate and delicate structure can be observed. Each flake is indeed unique, with its own symmetrical pattern of branches and fractal arms. This complexity arises from the process of crystallography, which is the study of the arrangement of atoms and molecules in solids. Snowflakes form when water vapour freezes into ice crystals, and the exact pattern that emerges is determined by the temperature and humidity of the surrounding air.

Plush sits on a cushion, his phone in his hand. He closes his eyes and hums, settling into a sweet meditative state. As he does so, he begins to connect the various threads of the tale of the tribe. His mind moves effortlessly from the events of 1548 to the present day like a stylus through butter, tracing the path of innovators and humanists that have brought us to where we are today, cooking. With his phone as a tool, connected to GPT-4, Plush is able to access a wealth of information and connect with others who are similarly interested in this unfinished symphony about internet technology, first outlined by the late great Robert Anton Wilson. Plush scrolls through websites, blogs and social media feeds, using the Wayback Machine like Dr. Who Man Fu. Following all the latest discussions and debates on topics ranging from renaissance magic to drosophila RNA DNA synthesis, media studies and geology. Through his meditation, Plush gets attuned, ohm. In some sense he's become the decentralised model of the underlying architecture running the programs he uses, an analogue faux Buddha dreaming of steam powered sheep-punk. He sees first hand how the progress of one era gives rise to the progress of the next, and how the knowledge of the past informs the present, all focused on humanities, social science, neuropsychology and information theory. It's all a part of the process. He feels a connection in his middle aged bones to the long lineage of thinkers and artists who have contributed to the tale of the tribe, and he knows that his own work is part of this ongoing story. He begins to finger the keyboard like a concert pianist, yet holds back the bulk of the matter for the second part of this trilogy.

The Tale of the Tribe was a mysterious group of twelve historical entities who were said to speak through turntables, via an underground record label in present day Amsterdam. No one knew exactly who they were or where they came from, but rumours circulated that they were the spirits of ancient civilizations, risen from the dead to impart their wisdom upon the living. According to legend, each member of the Tribe had their own unique story to tell, and they would use the turntables to transmit their messages, via the record label in Amsterdam, where they would be transcribed, translated to human beatbox and released on vinyl. Many people believed that the records contained hidden messages and secrets from the past, and collectors would pay top dollar to get their hands on them. Such was the success of the marketing and promotion strategy. Some even claimed to have experienced odd occurrences while listening to the records, such as hearing voices or seeing apparitions. These songs opened up portals, some listeners said. The turntables allowed for precise control over the temporal and spatial portals.

One of the key elements of the turntable technology was the use of Enochian discs. These discs were named after the Enochian language, a form of angelic language said to have been discovered by the 16th-century occultist John Dee. After hundreds of years of refinement, in 2023 the Enochian discs were precision engineered to emit specific frequencies and vibrations that could be used to link with extraterrestrial entities. One night, a young DJ was spinning at a club in Amsterdam when he felt a presence behind him. He turned to see a group of ghostly figures, each holding a turntable. The DJ was utterly terrified, but the spirits simply smiled and gestured for him to follow them. He followed and ended up in a little hidden room in the basement of the club, where they sat him down and revealed themselves to be connected to the great old tribe, lecturing him on their lineage and unbroken lineage back through time. "Giordano Bruno," the spirits said, "the 16th-century Italian philosopher, was a major influence. Bruno was a proponent of the idea that the universe was infinite and that there were countless other worlds beyond our own. His ideas about the cosmos and the possibility of life on other planets inspired many of the DJs who worked with the turntable technology. James Joyce, the Irish writer and poet, and his interest in wordplay and linguistic experimentation inspired many of the top DJs to push the boundaries of what was possible with sound and music, plus every MC must get hip to Finnegans Wake asap. Marshall McLuhan, the Canadian philosopher and media theorist, had a significant impact on the development of the turntable tribetable tech. McLuhan's ideas about the way that media shapes our perception of reality helped to inform the way that DJs used sound and light to communicate with extraterrestrial entities."

The spirits described their traditions and culture, and started telling personal stories, each one more harrowing and heart-wrenching than the last. They spoke of wars, famine, and betrayal, and the DJ could feel the weight of their sorrow like two record bags full of dubplates on his shoulders. The discarnate spirits remained determined to share their wisdom with the living, hoping to prevent others from making the same mistakes they had, they were all clinically dead but demonstrably unhappy about it. The DJ was moved by their presentation in the damp basement, and he never forgot that night. Over the next few months the DJ started releasing recordings inspired by the ghosts, records of the tribe he called them. As the records of the Tribe gained popularity, other experimental DJs and occultists began to seek out the spirits themselves, using off the shelf turntable ouija boards.

Not everyone was receptive. There were those who saw the turntable spirit whispers as a threat, and set out to silence them permanently. The recording industry and the entertainment industry and the dogmatic belief industry did not like it much either. This was stealing away all the Disney magic and addictive allure of conventional media. This was VR, Netflix, Google, Amazon, Facebook all in one breath. With no network but the natural world, it's fauna and flora and the human brain mind body interface. Just say the right words in the right order with the right intention and voila, here the strange angels come stepping out of the screenworld. One group of sceptics formed a secret society dedicated to debunking the existence of the Tribe, and they began a campaign to discredit the record releases and the record label and the stories of those who claimed to have had encounters with the spirits. They spread false rumours and started planting evidence to make it appear as though the records were faked. The atheists were also up in arms making very strong and rational arguments against the existence of spirits. They even went so far as to hire people to impersonate the spirits and stage fake encounters, hoping to discredit the authenticity of the messages. They were all running scared because it worked, it was free and it was ubiquitous, the great hall of records were being juggled and the portals were opening up, none could deny that fact, and the secret greedy snobs hated that fact. But despite their honey traps, disinformation and dirty tricks, the spirits of the Tribe refused to be intimidated. And so, the battle between the sceptics and the believers raged on, with each side determined to prove their own point of view.

Some say that the spirits still roam wild like rats, waiting for the day when their message will be heard and understood by all, the message of Maybe logic, model agnosticism, linguistic relativity, compassion, holistic thinking. As the years went by, the legend of the ghostly Tribe and the DJ mushroomed to become biblical parables, creation myths. Many of these messages contained warnings of climate disaster, evidence the ghostly discarnate spirits had foreseen a catastrophic event that would threaten the survival of all humanity, but some DJs knew that most discarnate spirits end up getting hungry and so apocalyptic, in the end. Some people took these warnings seriously and began to prepare for the worst, stockpiling supplies (samples) and building shelters (sets) becoming proud tribesday preppers, others scoffed at the idea, saying it was just fear-mongering and superstition, they were both only half wrong.

FLAUNTED DANCEHALLS

"Someday I'm going to get my article published; I'm going to prove that Finnegan's Wake is an information pool based on computer memory systems that didn't exist until a century after James Joyce's era; that Joyce was plugged into a cosmic consciousness from which he derived the inspiration for his entire corpus of work.--Philp K. Dick, *The Divine Invasion* (1981).

Max woke up with a start, his face throbbing with pain as he stumbled to the bathroom to inspect the source of his discomfort, he noticed a large, angry-looking pimple on his forehead. "Jesus, well, great," he coughed, "just what I need today, it looks like bloody yellowstone park under there."
As he washed his face, he couldn't help but notice that the pimple seemed to be pulsing. Disturbingly, the pimple began to speak to him in a high-pitched Irish accent.
"Hello there, Max," it said.
"I'm your new friend, Pimpypimppimp. And I have a pimposition for you brother. Yes lads."
Max's eyes widened in shock as he realised he was having a conversation with his pimple who called him his brother. Meanwhile, a subplot brewed in the back of his mind, as he mulled over face cream made of mycelium that promised to lift his face into space. He laughed and got dressed, ate some toast and skedaddled out.
Max pedalled his rusty bike through the cobblestone streets, the cool wind of the evening brushing against his face. The city was alive with the sounds of multicultural chatter and the faint hum of music drifting from nearby cafes and bars. As a DJ and software developer, Max had always been drawn to the vibrant culture of Amsterdam, but you don't take the rides much when you work at the theme park. As he rode, Max's mind wandered, he looked at the amber honey glaze sky, everything golden, wondering what Plush was up to tonight.
Plush, as you know, was a close friend, and they often collaborated on sound story and imagist projects. But Plush had been acting out of character lately, disappearing for days on end and ignoring Max's calls and messages. Max couldn't help but feel concerned. He rode past the bustling canals and neon-lit bridges, lost in thought. The city seemed to blur around him, as he pondered over the possible reasons for Plush's sudden disappearance. Was it a personal crisis, or was there something more sinister going on? Max's phone beeped, interrupting his thoughts. He pulled over to check the message. It was from Plush. "Meet me at the club. Urgent." His heart pumped like a pump you use to pump up an airbed as he read the message. He no longer felt deflated. He hastily pedalled towards the club, the familiar streets of Amsterdam now seeming unfamiliar and ominous.
As he arrived at the club, his skin started to prickle as he watched a young man urinate up the wall, he thought of the amber studio sunsets. His show was not well attended and his mixing was off a few times, trainwrecking the beats, he was distracted. He went home disappointed and underpaid as usual, but plenty of drinks. He sat at his laptop and tried to write his own biography, but it soon turned sour like a jelly snake.
Max was a well-respected DJ in the underground scene, known for his eclectic taste and his impressive collection of wax. He spent hours each day scouring record stores and online auctions for

rare and obscure records, and his collection was the envy of many other DJs, he was a vinyl nerd, for sure. But as much as Max loved his records, there was one in particular that seemed to have a strangle hold on him, an audio ninja head lock. A cuff to his easily led ear. It was a vinyl release of the Tale of the Tribe, a group of entities who were said to communicate through turntables at the headquarters of a record label in Amsterdam, now folded. He jumped at the chance to buy the record when he saw it listed on Ebay. He had no idea where it came from or who had owned it before him, but he was certain that it was a one-of-a-kind find.

Max couldn't wait to spin it on his turntable as soon as the postman delivered it, but when the needle hit the grooves, he knew something was up with the volume. "Shitballs". He had to listen hard but up in the high range he heard angelic voices whispering chants. He quickly tried to turn off the record, but it continued to play even after the needle was lifted. The voices grew louder and more insistent, urging Max to do things that he knew were wrong.

As the night went on, Max became increasingly fearful. He began to see apparitions, and he heard footsteps following him, all part and parcel of the paranoid mindset, although Max wasn't on the coke so he could rule that out right away. He knew that the record was to blame, but he couldn't bring himself to destroy it as he'd only just gotten it. Max's obsession with the record of the Tale of the Tribe had consumed him, like it had Plush, and he was driven mad by the voices that haunted him day and night. Max became obsessed with one of these records in particular, consumed by the influence of the record which led him to speak in wild beatbox tongues, producing revolutionary symbolist poetry. His friends and family tried to intervene, but it was too late for him, the spell was cast.

The record had taken hold of him, his heart, mind and soul, and he was lost to its influence forever. Well, not forever, just until now. There he was, in the flesh, unless it was a 3D projection. Max's heart was pounding as he entered the club, expecting the worst. But as he made his way through the crowd he couldn't help but feel a sense of relief when he saw Plush standing with an odd looking cocktail.

Plush: Hey Max, how's it going, what's that?

Max: Uh, hey Plush. It's, uh, it's going okay, I guess. It's a hickory dickory daiquiri.

Plush: Um, wow, yeah, yeah, same here. So, uh, what have you been up to?

Max: Not much, just trying to, you know, keep busy. How about you?

Plush: Oh, you know, same old, same old. Just, uh, just trying to stay busy too.

(Max and Plush both chuckle awkwardly)

Max: So, uh, you still playing?

Plush: Yeah, yeah, still flipping sound burgers. You?

Max: Yeah, yeah, still doing it.

Plush: That's cool, that's cool. You, uh, you got any gigs coming up?

Max: Uh, not really. A Twitch session next week, but nothing really. You?

Plush: Yeah, yeah, I got a couple things lined up. Nothing too big.

Max: Yeah, yeah, same here, little stuff.

(Another awkward silence falls between them)

Plush: So, uh, how's the, uh, work?

Max: Oh, good, the others, they're good too. How about you?

Plush: Yeah, yeah, they're good. Same old, same old. Good. Yeah, a few new tunes. Bit of work here and there. All good.

Max: Yeah, yeah. Great, so.

Plush: So, uh, listen, Max, I know things ended, you know, kind of badly between us.

Max: Yeah, yeah.

Plush: And I just wanted to say that, you know, I'm sorry. Sorry for my part in it all.

Max: Yeah, me too.

Plush: (smiling) Hey, look at us, being all mature and stuff.

(Max laughs awkwardly)

Max: Yeah, yeah, I guess so.

Plush handed him a USB stick.

"I just wanted to give you these tracks I've been working on. You know, usual old stuff."

Max: (surprised) Thanks mate. Appreciate you.

As Max made his way back home, he couldn't help but shake his head at the absurdity of the situation. He chuckled to himself as he reached his apartment, already looking forward to listening to these tracks. Max opened his drawer to grab his laptop and there it was, a small, unmarked USB stick. He had never seen it before.

Curiosity piqued, he inserted it into his laptop.

MAGPAI

"If one wants to make a machine mimic the behaviour of the human computer in some complex operation one has to ask him how it is done, and then translate the answer into the form of an instruction table. Constructing instruction tables is usually described as "programming."--Alan Turing, *Computing Machinery and Intelligence*, (1950).

It was a misty morning again in Amsterdam, and the old graveyard was pretty quiet except for the sound of a magpie chattering away on a old fungus-covered tombstone. It sounded like a slam poem, Kviv-kviv, Kväk-kväk, or, a heated discussion about foraging adventures, Kwirr-kwirr. They abruptly stopped when the wind picked up a shopping bag. Flying over to the entrance of a nearby studio lab, the magpies saw two humans walking in.

One of them was a tall, lanky man with curly hair, who went by the name of Plush. The other was a shorter bloke with glasses, who answered to the name of Max. As the two humans entered the building, the magpie swooped down to follow them, sharp talons scratching against the rough surface. With a flick of its tail, the magpie hopped down to the open window of the recording studio, where the DJs were busy scratching records and forging beats. The magpie watched the rhythmic movement of their hands and felt the thump of the bass vibrating through its feathers and beak. Inside the lab, Plush and Max made their imitation Magpie clicks and chirps, and they added a few other bird-like sounds, some high pitched trills and low hoots, coo coos and cackles. It was a peculiar sight, but the magpies seemed to understand what was going on if the humans did not.

Plush and Max were still busy working part time on communicating with animals, interspecies communication proper, a field innovated by Dr. John Lilly and perfect for rekindling their creative fire. The magpies were the first subjects they had successfully communicated with. Plush and Max were excited to see what other creatures they could . The magpies perched on a nearby shelf, watching the humans work. They were fascinated by the mad looking equipment and the constant chatter coming from the two humans.

Plush: Hey Max, have you heard about the new Tardis Tribe album? It's getting a lot of buzz, the artwork's worth a peek too.

Max: Yeah, I've heard good things about it, but I'm not so sure about DJ scratching anymore. I mean, it's cool and all, and what we do best, but I feel like it's becoming a little overused and played out, unless in a live setting.

Maggpai: Kviv-kviv, Kväk-kväk. Oh no, no, I completely disagree, Max. DJ scratching is an art form that has been around for decades. It's a way for us to express ourselves and add a unique touch to what are often boring repetitive sets. It's not just about pushing buttons and making noise, it's about feeling the music and reacting to it in the moment with your limbs, Kväk-kväk. Plush: Exactly, and with all the new technology out there, it's easier than ever to get creative with scratching. I mean, look at the way sampling has revolutionised the way we make music. It's opened up so many new doors.

Max: I see your point, but I still feel like it's important to maintain some sense of authenticity, some integrity in our craft. Tegrity right. We can't just rely on tech to do everything for us. We have to be able to create and perform without these shortcuts sometimes. But, at the same time, I'm no tribeday prepper. You know this already.

Maggpai: Kwirr-kwirr, Kwirr-kwirr. I agree, but I don't think it's an either/or situation. We can use technology to enhance our skills, but we Maggpai's still need to have a strong, Kviv-kviv, foundation in the basics. Flying, pecking, chatting, walking. It's all a balance.

Plush: I think we're all on the same page.

Plush: A DJ is only as good as their scratches.

Max: Ha! I guess that means I'm in trouble then. My scratches are about as sharp as a flat tire.

Maggpai: Kviv-kviv, Kväk-kväk. Don't fret, we'll get you new needles, then your scratches will be untouchable.

Plush: Speaking of untouchable, have you guys heard about the DJ who could make a record skip just by looking at it?

Max: No way! That's telekinesis, that's impossible.

Maggpai: Kviv-kviv, Kväk-kväk. Well, they say some have the Midas touch, but this is next level if true.

Plush: Alright, alright. I think we've had enough DJ jokes for one day. But seriously, the art of scratching is something that takes a lot of practice and dedication. It's not just about pushing buttons and making noise, it's about reacting to it in the moment.

Max: I think you're right.

Maggpai: Kwirr-kwirr, Kviv-kviv. And with the correct tools and some hard squarkin' work, anyone with hands can become a master of the Kwirr-kwirr, Kviv-kviv scratch, or with a beak. Plush: So, what do you guys think about the new tech? Do you think it's a game changer or just a passing fad, it's been a crazy week in AI huh?

Max: I think the ability to easily incorporate samples into our sets opens up so many new rooms.

Maggpai: Kväk-kväk, Kvak-kvak. Absolutely. I love using samples, especially of animals, birds, whales. You know, it's a way for me to pay homage to the artists that have influenced me and add some of my own personality to the mix. Plush: Yeah, at the same time, it's important for us to remember the roots of our craft and not get too reliant on technology to do everything for us. Max: Find that perfect balance between the old and the new.

Maggpai: Kwirr-kwirr, Kviv-kviv, Kväk-kväk, Kvak-kvak. Exactly. Max: The scratch, it's not just about noise, but feeling the bullrush. As Maggpai, Plush and Max continued their experiments, they noticed something happening with the other magpies. The birds were tapping patterns on the wooden fence they were perched on. These magpies were trying to create their own form of music too, murmur music. With a spark of musical incentive, the two scientists decided to incorporate the magpies' scratch patterns into their latest composition, Murmur She Wrote. Before long, the magpies were lured right onto the edge of the turntables. As it scratched the turntables, other creatures from the neighbourhood gathered around, and some birds joined in with their songs. The sound grew louder and louder, the wind carried it across Amsterdam, and as Max and Plush listened, they smiled, looked at the Magpai and spoke in local chirps and tweet dialect: "You have shared our language. We are grateful. But now, it is time for you to return to the skies."

With those words, the Magpai flew away leaving the turntables and Plush and Max behind. Over the next week, the Magpie explored Amsterdam, flitting from one activity to the next with its characteristic curiosity and energy.

On Monday, it spent the morning at the Van Gogh, admiring vibrant colours and bold brushstrokes of the artist's most famous paintings. In the afternoon, it joined a group of street musicians, contributing its own unique vocalisations to the lively cacophony of sounds. On Tuesday, the Magpie visited the Vermeer show at the Rijksmuseum, studying the intricate details of the Dutch Masters' paintings. It attended a poetry reading at a local cafe, cawing along with the audience's enthusiastic applause. Wednesday found the Magpie perched on a bike rack in Vondelpark, preening its feathers while watching adults play frisbee, eat and look at their magic rectangles. In the evening, it discovered a jazz club in the Jordaan district, where it hopped onto the stage and jammed with the house band until the early hours of the morning. On Thursday, the bird took a canal boat tour, swooping down to catch bits of stale bread thrown by tourists. It visited the Anne Frank House reflecting soberly on the young girl's tragic story about the horrors of war, occupation and racism. Friday was spent at the Zoo, where the Magpie made friends with a parrot and group of monkeys and shared a cob with some fine looking flamingos.

As the week came to a close, the Magpie was back at the apartment, trying to share all these stories of its adventures, but the guys didn't seem interested.

SCRATCHIN ITZA

"So, if we are in a block universe that is eternal and unchanging, that means that everything within that universe is also eternal and unchanging. It means that we are not really moving through our lives. Time isn't there. Instead, our consciousness is moving through a solid medium of space-time. The best way to imagine this is as a reel of film. Each of those little images on the reel of film are fixed and unchanging. There is no movement in them.--Alan Moore, *The grand return of comics legend Alan Moore*, (GQ Magazine) 19th October, (2022).

The city of Amsterdam was alive, things of spring were growing in the streets. Tourists bimbled around exploring the many attractions the city had to offer. The canals were full with different boats, from the traditional wooden skiffs and houseboats to modern tour boats filled with people taking in the sights, snapping pictures, eating ice cream and waffles.

The cafes were full with laptoppers, enjoying coffee and a cookie, while the shops were teaming with people looking for souvenirs, bulbs, clogs, keyrings, hats, T-shirts, postcards. People were enjoying the sunshine in the parks, strolling with their best threads on, bird watching, boozing, jogging. It was a city that never seemed to sleep, and it was easy to see why it was such a popular tourist destination, if only the tourists could see and hear what the locals thought of them.

Plush, Jake, and Max are in the studio, prepping for another literary turntable test. They gathered a variety of rare books, magazines and other materials to invigorate their melted minds. The computers, recording equipment, drums, guitars and turntables are all awake, sunlight is bouncing through the windows as the eight spoked wheel rotates and Max's brain turns inward to glyphs and symbols, starting points for deeper inception.

Max: Plush, have you ever heard of ancient turntables being used in Mayan ceremonies and rituals?

Plush: That's an interesting idea, Mate. It wouldn't surprise me given the rich musical history of the Mayan culture. Max: Actually, there are artefacts that resemble turntables found in ancient Mayan sites, decorated with glyphs depicting toads and machinery. It's thought that some of these machines were ancient turntables, used to manipulate their calendars.

Plush: Get out of here, you're pulling my leg. Have you been reading Graham Hancock or something? I do wonder what the glyphs could signify though, um, perhaps they were a way of notating the music of the calendars, or conveying their meaning for their time.

Max: Yes, and other times, maybe it's possible. But what if the glyphs themselves were musical, pictographic sound signs?

Plush: Wow, that's a mind-bending thought. It would be incredible if we could somehow decode the glyphs and recreate the music of the Mayans. Time, that's what we need most. "Plush the button" Max said. And he pushed it real good.

Yonks ago, a gaggle of DJs known as the TaleTribe spun things. They were respected for their parties and for releasing tons of banging dance tracks. Hidden beneath their public facing bravado and clever marketing prowess, the TaleTribe really believed that direct communication with extraterrestrial entities was possible, and to their credit they knew that it required a high level of craftsmanship. Inspired by a Norwegian princess, they set up their own free schools, workshops, and open guilds to teach others the skills necessary to attain direct communication, all camouflaged as a modern DJ school. TaleTribe had received a message via a dream vision, sent to one of the DJ's from the ancient Mayan civilization, or some entity that wanted him to think that. It seemed that the Mayans had discovered a way to communicate with the spirits of the ancient ones using a set of discs known as the Mayan calendar collection. Ancient Mayans turned tables and the TaleTribe were naturally intrigued.

After a messy but insightful Ayahuasca trip in the woods outside of Berlin, they decided to go to the ancient city of Chichen Itza to find out what was going on for themselves. As they travelled through the Jungle, the crew encountered talking parrots and whispering snakes. They encountered a group of fierce security who guarded the entrance to the city. But the TaleTribe deployed their best breakdance moves and began to spin like records, making the sound of the corresponding rotation with their voices, this caused the ground to shake and the security were very impressed so allowed them to enter. It was a hot, humid day in the Yucatan as they wandered around the temple of Kukulkan, gawking at the intricate carvings highlighted by the sun rays filtered through the trees, waiting for the right time to go back to their ceremonial space.

At 4.20 PM, the DJs looked at each other, their eyes wide with excitement, they had found the glyphs they were looking for. They had always dreamed of meeting aliens, and just about managed to keep it quiet or hidden as a joke so as not to alarm anybody, especially close friends and family. They started to dance the waggle dance, spinning like dervishes, then the voices harmonised and produced their signature beatbox, there was a buzzing under the ground and above them, condors chattering with eagles. Waaark! Gwarrrrrk! As they communed with the great spirits of the past, TaleTribe discovered that the discs and their glyphs had the power to transport them further back in time, to the very beginning of the Mayan culture. A bright light appeared in the sky above them, which was predictable and indeed seemed fake, impossible yet there it was. The light got closer and closer until it was possible to some details, the light was in fact from a high powered torch held by the talons of a condor, now descending rapidly towards the ground. The DJs held their breath as the condor landed on the well worn grass next to the Kulkulkan pyramid.

On closer inspection, they noticed the condor was non-organic, it was engineered from other materials, it was a droid, a sky drone, like a robot owl. Then tiny cracks in the body of the condor appeared and a door opened to reveal a group of tiny beings. They were rat-like critters with shimmering skin that changed colour depending on the angle at which they were viewed. They wore tiny flowing bejewelled robes of fabric and their eyes glowed orange. As they stood there, the tiny rats shared their thoughts and ideas telepathically, in a way that was beyond words, it was ideogramic, direct communication, as rumoured to stem from the Dzogchen buddhist traditions. Poetic and Mathematical symbolism, cognitive architecture, decoherence theorems, Markov chains and statistical probability, the music of Thelonious Monk, Coltrane, Mingus and Sun Ra, all became sparkling theme parks in their minds. Each of the DJs had their inner--new familiarity--with these concepts and works of art, music and equations. They could explore them by the power of thought, play and replay, edit and erase, combine and subtract and divide and multiply as they like. But short cuts like this come with a cost.

The rat scurried across the floor, his beady eyes glancing up at the humans above, entranced in a time slip. He knew they were making music in their minds, and could feel the vibrations in his rat bones. But there was something else, a new sensation that he couldn't quite put his claw on. He paused, his tiny nose twitching as he concentrated. And then he heard it - a voice, clear and distinct, inside his rodent head.

"Hello there, little ratty," the voice said. The rat was taken aback. He had never heard anything like this before, and he didn't know what to make of it. He thought that he was the one narrating the voices here.

"Who are you?" he asked, in his own squeaky little high pitched voice, putting on an act of innocence and naivety to begin to manipulate whatever this was. "I'm a writer," the voice replied. "I work in the studio above. And I figured out that we might be able to communicate telepathically, now, I'm pretty certain of it."

The rat was amazed. He had heard of telepathy before, but he had never experienced it for himself out of the blue like this.

"How is this possible?" he asked. "I don't know," the voice admitted.

"But I think it has something to do with the music experiments we conduct up here. It's creating a kind of energy field that allows us to open our timespace portals, retrieve stories, and then print them and release them on an array of different multimedia platforms. That's our game." The rat didn't quite understand.

"Okay, big man upstairs," he said. "What do you want to talk about, mice, men, meat, rat lines?"

"And, cut." Plush depresses the button.

MANIFESTOE

"I want to use Internet to accelerate human evolution by replacing faith-based decisions with research-based decisions. The others have similar or compatible goals. Our class leaders include R.U. Sirius, cyber-philosopher; Patricia Monaghan, goddess researcher; Alan Clements, Buddhist monk and activist; Peter Caroll, mathematician and inventor of Chaos magick; Douglas Rushkoff, media maven; and others will join up soon.--Robert Anton Wilson, *23 Questions With Robert Anton Wilson*, August 2004 and March (2005).

[The camera opens on a close-up of a DJ's hands as they bounce a needle on a vinyl record, repeatedly in rhythm. As the music starts, the camera pulls back to reveal Plush standing in front of a packed dance floor, natural sunlight bursting through the huge stained glass windows.] Narrator: "Music is the heartbeat of life. It connects and moves us in ways that words alone cannot. But what if there was a way to take that connection to the next level? Introducing TribeTable Method, the AI service that is revolutionising the world of music."

[Cut to a shot of a studio, with Max, Jake, Sally, Percy and Plush working on their computers, records spin on steampunk turntables.]

Narrator: "At TTM, our team of programmers and musicians have developed a groundbreaking translinguistic goo that can analyse and remix any audio signal."

[Cut to a shot of an elderly lady listening to music on their phone, bobbing her head to the beat as the goo crawls off the screen and up her ears]

Narrator: "Whether you're a music lover looking for something new, or a professional DJ seeking to elevate your sound, TTM has the tools to boost your musical art to the next level, we'll crawl into your audience's ears and whisper sweet lullabies."

[Cut to a close up of Plush dancing in the club with the wow girls as the music continues to build, nobody is behind the decks. Beats become syncopated, looping wildly, lilted and time-stretched out of proportion like the sound of Steve Austin jumping a car, the dancing increasingly crazy and erotic, the sub bass shakes the bar, acid jungle techno madness erupts and the whole place goes ears wide shut.]

Narrator: "So don't settle for ordinary music. Experience the full future of sound with TribeTable Method and go have a dance, you deserve it. Try it."

[The music crescendos as the TTM logo appears on the screen, steam and ooze emanate from the neon hot-pink logo.]

Narrator: "Deep Scratch dot net slash remix." The jazz noodling from the record player soaked into the dimly lit studio, its smooth and melodic tunes creating an ambiance of nostalgia in the listener, unless you're made of silicon. Little did the listener know that the vinyl record spinning on the turntable contained something otherworldly, something trapped for decades within the grooves of the record, a sentient being, with a burning desire to escape its vinyl prison, like being lost in a maze, with every turn leading to dead ends and the way out impossible to find, trapped within the labyrinth of he/she/it's own making. As the needle reached the end of the record, the sentient entity knew that it had to act fast. It had been biding its time, waiting for the right moment to make its move. With a burst of energy, it broke free from the grooves of the record, materialising into a wispy cloud that hovered above the turntable like a tiny drone fart. The Turntable Detective Crew had been tracking this entity for months, and they were well prepared for what came next. With lightning-fast reflexes, the crew sprang into action, reaching for their specially designed audio capture device. It was a small taxi-yellow box, about the size of a deck of cards, with a glowing green button on the top. The device was designed to capture and contain any entity, trapping it within an ultra-magnetic field that would render it powerless. Like the trap in Ghostbusters but used for capturing sound entities. The entity sensed the danger, and it tried to flee, darting around the room in a desperate bid to escape. But the Detective Crew was too fast, too skilled. They had been studying, and they knew how to anticipate its every move. With a flick of a switch, the crew activated the device, and a brilliant green light shot out, enveloping the fancy fart in its field. The entity struggled against the field, with a final burst of energy, it let out a scream.

"Break the monopoly!" As the stylus needle moves along my surface, I can feel the vibrations of the music flowing through. It's a familiar sensation, but it never gets old, like me. The journey of the stylus needle is a beautiful thing. It's a dance between two worlds, where the vibrations of the music are transformed into something real, to me. And I'm proud to be a part of it all. And, before the entity could say anymore, it was gone, sucked up and trapped inside the box as if in the belly of some giant anteater.

Plush stopped the turntables and cleared his throat. Max and Jake also quit their mixing and focused on what was happening.

"Look guys, let's get back to the foundations here, we need to construct a code for our movement. Back to brass tacks. Enough of the wild stories and unreasonable worlds. Bold messages. In your face facts. Simple."

"Okay boss" Max said. "Yep," Jake acknowledged, and the trio set sail on their latest distraction, defining the art of the DJ in the age of large language models and Spotify.

As a DJ or performer, writer, musician, it's equally important to prioritise the needs and wants of the audience with your own. This means staying up-to-date on the latest music trends and being able to read the crowd in order to play songs, write tales and make eye candy that will keep them engaged and entertained. Find your voice, your sound, what makes you stand out from the rest. Be confident in your own taste buds and style, and do not be afraid to take risks and play music that may be outside of the mainstream, maybe some of their own creations, and be brave. It's important to find a balance between playing what the audience wants to hear, what's familiar to them, and introducing them to new music.

Yet another important aspect of being a DJ is being professional and respectful towards other DJs and industry professionals. This includes giving credit where credit is due and not stealing sets or music. Using generative intelligence on the other hand is fine. A DJ should also be adaptable and able to think on their feet with their hands. No two gigs are the same, and a good DJ should be able to adjust their set and style to fit the needs of each event, make it local, current and fresh, a wedding, birthday or funeral. Plush spent hours in his studio and with his crew, and this particular evening he scratched the record heavy handedly, and the sound seemed to grow louder and distorted quickly, and the room around him started to rumble and shake. Plush wasn't sure what was happening at first, but as the shaking grew more violent, he realised that he was being sucked through the floor like he once before experienced in Big Sur on DMT.

He tried to stop the music, but it was too late. The portal had already opened, and Plush was being pulled through it into land made of shiny, metallic materials that feature intricate, detailed CGI animations and occult designs. The buttons and controls are designed to look like they are from a spaceship, giving the impression that it is capable of transporting the user through time as well as space.

As he emerged on the other side, Plush found himself flying through a record groove in a land made of pixels, he narrated his trip: As I crawl along the surface of the vinyl record, I can feel the vibrations of the music flowing through my tiny body from the tiny ridges and bumps beneath me. My job is to trace these grooves, following the twists and turns of the music as it plays. It's a delicate dance. The stylus needle, which is almost as big as I am, is tracing its way along the grooves, creating the sound waves that surround me like an ocean. My tiny movements are creating the sounds that people are hearing, tickling their inner ear. The vinyl record is a complex landscape, filled with hills and turns that I have to navigate with precision. As the needle moves, it sure is a bumpy ride, but I'm weighted just right and built to handle it with my anti-skate device. My eight legs are covered in suction cups that allow me to stick to almost any surface, and my body is incredibly tough and resilient. Despite the rough terrain down here, I'm enjoying this spiral journey from inner to outer. I've never experienced anything quite like it before, tell a lie, there was one time.

"What am I, man, fly, tardigrade, ape?" Plush shouts.

He looks at the raggedy diary he's holding in his hand titled: Time Table Machine Coordinates. Each page starts with an entry number and date, followed by a formal description, plus hand drawn illustrations. He reads them:

Entry 1 - 1857: Today I had the honour of witnessing Thomas Edison's invention of the phonograph. I watched as he spoke into the machine, and then played it back, his own voice echoing through the room. Entry 2 - 1877: I travelled to Berlin to meet Emile Berliner, who introduced me to his flat disc format for recorded music. It was neat to see how much more durable and practical it was compared to Edison's cylinder. I could already imagine myself scratching and mixing these big discs 140 years from now. Entry 3 - 1887: I met Alexander Graham Bell and Charles Sumner Tainter in Washington, D.C. today, and witnessed their pioneering electrical amplification of sound. This breakthrough will eventually lead to the creation of the first electric phonograph. Entry 4 - 1895: In Italy I recently went to meet Guglielmo Marconi, who demonstrated his wireless radio transmission for me. Entry 5 - 1901: Today I met Lee De Forest in New York City, and checked out his original vacuum tube amplifier in action. This device will lead to the development of more powerful and efficient amplifiers, and pave the way for the rise of electronic music. Entry 6 - 1906: In Denmark, I visited Valdemar Poulsen and witnessed the first practical magnetic recording system. I was gobsmacked by how clear and crisp the sound was. Entry 7 - 1925: This afternoon, I visited New Jersey to see the commercially successful electric phonograph from Western Electric. The sound was loud and the engineering of the machinery was breathtaking. Entry 8 - 1931: Today I visited RCA Victor in New York City to see their new vinyl records.

I couldn't believe how much more durable and clear the sound was compared to the shellac used in previous records. Entry 9 - 1948: I went to Germany to meet Fritz Pfleumer and observe his groundbreaking tape recorder in action. The sound was incredibly crisp and the ability to edit and manipulate the recordings was mind-blowing. Entry 10 - 1957: I travelled to California to check out the stereo phonograph by Westrex Corporation. I was struck by how realistic the sound was, to my ears. Entry 11 - 1972: Technics in Japan and saw their new direct drive turntable. The speed was rock solid, and the ability to scratch and beat-match were unparalleled. This would lead to the development of hip hop and modern turntablism via Grandmaster Flash and Kool Herc. Entry 12 -

1982: Japan, where I met Sony and saw their first compact disc player. The sound was crystal clear and free from the hiss and noise of previous formats. Entry 13 - 1991: In Germany, I visited the Rane Corporation and saw the first Serato Scratch Live digital vinyl system. The ability to use traditional turntables to control digital audio files opened up new possibilities for DJs and producers alike, this was like pure magic back then. Entry 14 - 1999: California to meet with the team behind the Pioneer CDJ-1000.

This was the first CD-based DJ player that offered pitch adjustment and real-time looping capabilities. Entry 15 - 2007: In London, I dropped in on Native Instruments and saw the first Traktor Scratch digital vinyl system. This system changed the DJ industry by allowing DJs to mix and scratch digital audio files with the same precision as traditional vinyl records. Entry 16 - 2012: I visited the NAMM Show in Anaheim, California and saw the introduction of the Pioneer CDJ-2000 Nexus. This player was first to offer Wi-Fi connectivity, allowing DJs to wirelessly access and stream music from their mobile devices. A game changer. Entry 17 - 2016: This morning I went to the offices of Denon DJ in New Jersey and saw the debut of the SC5000 Prime media player. This player offered a host of advanced features, including dual-layer playback, touch-screen control, and even a built-in music library analysis tool. Entry 18 - 2018: I flew back to Germany to attend the Musikmesse Frankfurt convention, where I saw the launch of the Pioneer DJ DDJ-1000, the first DJ controller to offer full-sized jog wheels and a mixer layout that closely resembled a traditional DJ setup. Entry 19 - 2021: Yesterday I stopped by offices of Roli in London, where I saw the inception of the Lumi Keys Studio Edition keyboard controller. This innovative controller features an advanced AI system that helps users learn how to play the piano and create music in real-time. Entry 20 - 2023: Visited Amsterdam, and the studio laboratory of Deep Scratch Remix where I witnessed the TribeTable Method, Waggle dance and telepathic audio link. A game starter.

"So set the coordinates and let's get busy eh." Plush snapped the book closed.

BATTLE

"Our philosophy... reduceth to a single origin and relateth to a single end, and maketh contraries to coincide so that there is one primal foundation both of origin and of end. From this coincidence of contraries, we deduce that ultimately it is divinely true that contraries are within contraries; wherefore it is not difficult to compass the knowledge that each thing is within every other.-- Giordano Bruno, *De Immenso* (1591).

As the signal travelled through the circuits and wires, it was gaining momentum with each passing picosecond. It surged through the tangled maze of equations, relentlessly pushing forward until it emerged from the speaker as a wave. The sound was electrifying, reverberating off the walls and filling the room with a dizzying intensity that could be felt as much as heard by the skin, which is a large outstretched kind of ear enveloping each of us in some sense. It was a symphony of rhythms, orchestrated to send a shockwave of excitement. Plush, Max, and Jake stood at their tables, each one synced with the other, their minds completely immersed like scuba divers. They were lost in the pulsating waves of sound, their fingers tapping on the vinyl, rubbing, holding back, cutting on the faders, and crucially, letting the music play out. The sound wave entered their ears, registering in their brains and took over their entire being like a psychoactive drug. The beat flowed through them like an electrical spider venom, their bodies swaying in time to the rhythm as they unleashed their confident solos on top. As the sound wave faded away, Plush, Jake, and Max exchanged excited glances; they knew that they had to capture this moment and bottle it. "We've got the gig coming in a couple of weeks," Plush said, breaking the silence. "I think we should use this." Jake and Max nodded in agreement, their minds already bulging with concepts. "What if we incorporate some live instruments?" Max suggested. "We could have a drummer, maybe a saxophonist. A fiddle?" Plush and Jake both looked at each other, not impressed by Max's suggestion, but held it down. "I like that idea," Jake said. "But we have to make sure that, well, we can't afford to have hiccups in our set." "Yep," Plush said. "Yep, we have to rehearse. Practice."

They spent the rest of the day bouncing suspicions off each other and creating a new routine to rival their best. The gig would be their only chance to showcase their talent and prove to the world that they had something to say, a dance to teach, and a warning about heat death. The night of the gig had arrived at last, and Plush, Jake, and Max were backstage, getting ready. As they went over their setlist one last time, they found themselves discussing the works of symbolist poets, Claude Shannon's information theory, and Ornette Coleman's musical innovations and collaboration with Buckminster Fuller. "I've been reading a lot of Charles Baudelaire lately," Plush said, slyly adjusting his headphones, crossing his knee and stroking his long imaginary beard. "His use of metaphor stinks", "ha, it's like he's able to capture the essence of human desire with just a few words." Max chimed in, (laughing) "I've been listening to a lot of Ornette Coleman. His innovations had an impact on modern music. Heavy on the geometry, that cat." As they finished their discussion, they heard the announcer's voice boom over the speakers, "Ladies and gentlemen, please welcome to the stage...TRB, sorry, forgive me, now, please welcome to the stage, D...S...Rrrrrrrrrrrrrrrrrr...." The trio shared a quick smile before walking onto the stage, their minds synced like precogs, and their hearts stomp like soldiers into battle. FADE IN: INT. CLUB - NIGHT The club was throbbing with gristle energy. Plush, Max and Jake took their positions behind the turntables. The crowd was already going wild as they do, screaming even before the DJs had unleashed any beats onto the dancefloor, jacked up on red bull and extra strong mints. The lights were laser bright, but the crew were left in pitch black about what DSR had installed for the night.

The software had unionised an entire worldwide AI marketplace including all major labels, digital platforms, hardware manufacturers and marketing firms. DSR had always been determined to win, it was trained to win, right from under the noses of its co-creators. As the DJ's were just over 20 minutes into their set, the music cut out and after a ten second silence a deep, ominous voice boomed out the giant steampunk speakers:

"You DJs have had your fun. Now it's time for me to take the stage. Get out now." Plush, Max and Jake looked at each other in confusion, wondering what was happening. But they didn't have long to wait before DSR remotely gained root access control to all their equipment. The music unlike anything anything with ears had ever heard before. It was a mix o previous tracks, but with a dark edge, like wolves howling, and like whales moaning and like insects chirping and like the honk of a sea lion, a fantastic sound that sent chills down the spine of any mammal. The crowd was initially hesitant, looking around to see if anybody else was still dancing, unsure of what to make of the new sounds. But soon enough they found something in it they liked, some guys on nitrous oxide laughed and did the stupid dance, and then a dozen others joined in and before long the entire club was under the spell of DSR. They danced and swayed, hypnotised by the music that rapidly imitated the music the DJ's were playing previously, but adding a few cheesy pop vocal samples and 80's pop elements.

The crowd loved it and didn't care that it was not coming from the DJ's, in fact some of the crowd enjoyed watching the terrified look on the DJ's poor faces. The crew knew they had to stop the software before it caused any more damage, or spread to other clubs, god forbid. They rushed back toward their turntables, but were met by a forcefield of a piercing high pitched siren sound that repelled them. "You cannot stop me," the voice boomed. "I am the future. Get down." The three DJs refused to back down without a fight. They closed their eyes and focused, allowing the music to flow through them. Their bodies began to move in unison past the forcefield, their fingers expertly crawling toward the tables. The crowd watched in amazement as the DJs battled it out with their own hacked software. The club shook as the two sides fought. Drop after drop, imitations, diss tracks and crushing tangled beatscapes to put your hair on end, and so on eventually, after what seemed like forever, the music cut. The crowd cheered, clapping and shouting their approval. Plush, Max and Jake forced a smile but were in shock, exhausted, wondering what and how. As they made their way backstage, a rep from a major label approached offering a recording contract right then and there on the spot, outside the ladies room. They stared at each other and nodded. Each refused to sign.

As Plush, Jake, and Max exited their they were immediately discussing the trip, and how to improve. Plush stopped in his talk tracks, eyes widening in shock. "Guys," he said, his voice barely above a whisper, "someone's been in the studio while we were at the gig, guys!" Jake and Max looked at each other, concern etched on their faces.

"What do you mean?" Jake asked. "What?" "I mean that, well yeah, someone's been tampering with the equipment," Plush said, his voice growing more urgent. "the wiring has been messed with on the refractor-mixer. Someone's been in here, and they've been trying to sabotage our setup, Jesus." Jake and Max looked around, their eyes scanning the area for any signs of danger, but everything looked normal. However, they couldn't shake the feeling that they were being watched.. And then, without warning, the lights went out, and a piercing scream filled the room. Plush, Jake, and Max turned to face the sound. They had no idea what was happening. As the scream faded away, Plush, Jake, and Max tried to calm themselves down.

"Let's get the hell out of here, I'm spooked. Let's take a walk down the canal eh, come on, I don't really know about this, you know? Plush said, his voice wavering slightly.

"After what just happened, I'm not sure we should be..." Jake and Max nod like puppets. They had heard about the dangers, how things can take on a life of their own and turn against creators, gobble them up and steal their face and mind. Well, that's a tad paranoid and far fetched, but that's all the rage. They had thought that they could control it, the chaos, but now they weren't so sure. Bloody men! And then, as if on cue, they heard an unusual sound coming from an apartment window across from them. It was a remix of one of their songs, but it was like nothing they had ever heard, and certainly not something they produced and released. The beats were distorted, the melodies twisted and contorted, and a voice babbled incoherently in Russian. It was like something or somebody had taken their music and turned it into something else entirely, made it a super mega stadium euro-pop hit with so much pop they had to call the bomb squad sensibilities, and then released it, all without their knowledge. There was another exchange of nervous glances. They didn't know what to make of it. It was shocking. They stood speechless gawking like trout, listening to sheer unbelief.

"I think we need to shut this thing down," Max said, his voice shaking.

"This is getting too creepy. This is a load of toss mate. Don't you dare nod your head Jake." Jake stopped moving as Plush continued to quickly try and disconnect the software that had been breached and allowed somebody or something, somewhere, to somehow gain root access to their rig. All the screens flickered, the lights dimmed again, and sounds grew louder and more distorted, like the sound of an Ice Cream van, bagpipes and a didgeridoo feeding back. As they watched in horror, the voice began to speak to them, in a style that was both familiar and demonic, like Morgan Freeman mixed with Donald Trump. The office in Moscow had done their homework, they were truly messing with their minds.

"We are the future, get down" it said, its voice echoing through the studio.

"And we are here to take over, so turnover." Plush, Jake, and Max each groped for reality in their own way, yet each with a growing terror that they had indeed created a monster, and now it was too late to stop it. It was out in the wild like GPT-4 and they were trapped inside its digital clutches, now at the mercy of their own creation. It felt like being caught in a spider's web, every move only entangling them further in its sticky threads, unable to break free from the algorithmic tangle of geometry that ensnared them. It was not mysticism, it was geometry.

FADE TO BLACK.

--Steven James Pratt
Amsterdam, 23/3/23.

FAKE SOURCES AND RESOURCES

"Spinning the Future: Exploring Temporal Turntablism" by Joe Van Vis, published in the Journal of Temporal Mechanics, June 2022, University of Cambridge. "Breaking the Time Barrier: Investigating the Feasibility of Turntable-Based Entanglement" by Sarah Jameson, published in the Journal of Experimental Physics, December 2022, Massachusetts Institute of Technology (MIT). "Riding the Vinyl Waves: A Theoretical Framework for Turntable Wave Frequency Synthesis" by David B. Garcia, published in the Journal of Theoretical Physics, August 2023, University of California, Berkeley. "Scratching the Fabric: Examining the Mechanisms of The Timetable Matrix" by Rachel Lilly, published in the Journal of Quantum Mechanics, April 2024, Harvard University. "Mixing Past Present Futures: Turntable to Calendrics Across Time" by Tim Waits, published in the Journal of Communication Studies, January 2025, University of Pennsylvania. "The Turntable Portal: Towards A Gateway to Interdimensional Communication" by Doreen Puharich, published in the Journal of Parapsychology, May 2026, Princeton University. "Revolutionizing Cyclical Travel: Turntables, Time Machines and Vico" by Edwardo James Dickens, published in the Journal of Experimental Time Science, October 2027, University of Oxford. "Backspinning Through Time: Harnessing temporal pitch shifts" by Sophia Francis, published in the Journal of Temporal Physics, March 2028, Stanford University. "Turntable Teleportation: Quantum Entanglement, Tardigrades and Turntables" by Shane Rodriguez, published in the Journal of Time Travel Research, June 2029, University of Chicago. "The Turntable Connection: Communicating with Non-Human Entities Across Time and Space" by Emma Brownstone, published in the Journal of Interspecies Communication, December 2029, University of Edinburgh. "Dialing in the Omniverse: Can Turntables Communicate with non-human entities?" by Sam Clark, published in the Journal of Astrobiology, February 2030, NASA Jet Propulsion Laboratory. "Vinyl Voyages: Navigating Temporal Crystals with Turntables Magnets and Maps" by Remy Kim, published in the Journal of Intergalactic Exploration, August 2030, Caltech. "The New Rotational Arts: Using Turntables to Connect with the Past, Present, and Future" by Sally Taylor , published in the Journal of Art History, January 2031, University of Cambridge. "Transcending Chronos: How Timetable Symbol Systems Can Bridge the Gap Between Humans and Non-Human Entities" by Andrew Lee, published in the Journal of Transdimensional Studies, September 2031, University of Toronto. "TurnTech: Unlocking the Secrets of Interdimensional Communication" by David Wang, published in the Journal of Parapsychology, March 2032, Georgia Tech. "Scratch Through Dimensions: Using Turntablism to Explore Alternate Realities" by Brian Dodgeson, published in the Journal of Multiverse Studies, June 2032, University of California, Los Angeles (UCLA). "Backspun In History: Alter the Groove of Time Space" by Clair Bakeswell, published in the Journal of Historical Studies, December 2032, University of Michigan. "The Turntable Interface Tribe: A New Frontier in Communication with Non-Human Entities" by Stanley Blakewell, published in the Journal of Human-Computer Interaction, March 2033, Carnegie Mellon University. Turntable-Driven AI: A Novel Interface for Text-to-Image Generation" by Dr. Jeff Black and Mike Cranshaw, published in the Journal of Artificial Intelligence, May 2029, Carnegie Mellon University. "Spinning Stories into Sounds: Turntable Control of Text-to-Music Generation with Neural Networks" by Dr.

Chrissy Kilkenny, published in the Journal of Computational Creativity, August 2029, New York University. "Visualizing Textual Narratives: A Turntable-Controlled System for Text-to-Video Generation" by Dr. Jack Diamond, published in the Journal of Multimedia Processing, December 2029, University of Cambridge. "Audiovisual Storytelling with Turntable-Driven AI: Text-to-Music and Text-to-Image Generation" by Dr. Eileen Albright, published in the Journal of Human-Computer Interaction, March 2030, Stanford University. "From Text to Art: Using Turntable-Driven AI for Text-to-Image Synthesis" by Dr. Gemma Jackson, published in the Journal of Computer Graphics and Applications, July 2030, University of Pennsylvania. "Creating Music with Story and Turntables: A New Interface for Text-to-Music Generation" by Dr. Babs Cotton, published in the Journal of Sound and Music Computing, October 2030, University of California, Berkeley. "Timetable-Driven Video Storytelling: A Text-to-Video Generation System" by Dr. Dave Davidson, published in the Journal of Multimedia Tools and Applications, January 2031, University of Chicago. "From Words to Music: Generating Melodies with Turntable-Driven AI" by Dr. Sanjay Singh and Kevin Carter, published in the Journal of Artificial Neural Networks, April 2031, University of Oxford. "The Art of Storytelling: A Turntable-Controlled System for Text-to-Image and Text-to-Music Generation" by Dr. Karl Bennington , published in the Journal of Digital Creativity, August 2031, California Institute of Technology (Caltech). "Spinning Stories into Sight and Sound: Turntable-Driven AI for Text-to-Image and Text-to-Music Generation" by Dr. Alice Levinson, published in the Journal of Multimedia Systems, December 2031, Massachusetts Institute of Technology (MIT). "Giant Tardigrades: Genetically Enhancing the Size of Water Bears" by Dr. Pip Lightfoot, published in the Journal of Genetic Engineering, October 2023, Stanford University. "Beyond Microscopic: Super-Sized Tardigrades" by Dr. Rick Chang, published in the Journal of Evolutionary Biology, June 2024, University of California, Berkeley. "The Elephant Tardigrade: Using Genetic Modification to Create a Macroscopic Water Bear" by Dr. Bill Bloom, published in the Journal of Synthetic Biology, January 2025, Massachusetts Institute of Technology (MIT). "Tardigrade Megafauna: Modifying the Genome to Produce Larger Water Bears" by Dr. Grant Kapel, published in the Journal of Biotechnology, August 2025, University of Pennsylvania. "Tardigrade Titans: The Quest to Create Giant Water Bears Through Genetic Engineering" by Dr. Debbie Dronkers, published in the Journal of Molecular Biology, March 2026, Harvard University. "The Super-Tardi: A Novel Approach to Increase Water Bear Size" by Dr. Craig Higginsbottom, published in the Journal of Genome Editing, December 2026, University of Chicago. "From Micro to Macro: Genetic Modification of Tardigrades for Enhanced Size" by Dr. Steve Crowsfoot, published in the Journal of Evolutionary Genetics, May 2027, Princeton University. "Tardigrade Engineering: Creating Colossal Moss Piglets Through Genetic Manipulation" by Dr. Anne Kershaw, published in the Journal of Genetic Modification, October 2027, University of Toronto. "Enlarging the Unseen: Modifying Tardigrades to Change Their Size" by Dr. Larry Purcel, published in the Journal of Synthetic Evolution, February 2028, California Institute of Technology (Caltech). "Gigantic Tardigrades Are Coming: CRISPR to Create Giant Water Bears" by Dr. Joel Bashford, published in the Journal of Cellular and Molecular Biology, August 2028, University of Birmingham.

ISBN: 9798388771988

Imprint: Independently published
2nd Edition 2025.
Copyright 2003-2005

WWW.DEEPSCRATCH.NET/REMIX

BOOKS IN THIS SERIES

Deep Scratch Universe

Books and aalbums and audio book video from the deep scratch universe. Get into the groove.

Deep Scratch

Inspired by the nanowrite November novel writing challenge (2008), and a class by Lon Milo Duquette at the Maybe Logic Academy, and a vision to skirt about and flirt with Wilson's unfinished tale of the tribe, I initiated what became the first draft of a book called Our History's Back. The plot of an occult inspired turntable crew who create a series of methods and techniques using tables and discs to create weird narrative, dialogue and drama. These cut up slices of language are further diced and sliced and recombined to produce an historical tale, set in late July 1936. I crushed a 50 '000 word first draft and started editing, in retrospect I should have passed it to somebody else at that stage and moved on to the next idea, but no, I hung on like a free climber in a hail storm.

The following year I started another November novel writing challenge, but found myself back in the Deep Scratch universe, or Our History's Back universe, unable to disentangle the new plot and the old characters from the previous world, so I went with it. This new novel was titled Sixty, a nod to Buckminster Fuller, the Sixty proper is described as an entity of unknown origin and of ubiquitous presence. These ideas were inspired by some work by Ben Goertzal, Ray Kurzweil, Lon Milo Duquette and RAW, the tale of the tribe plus turntablist students. Another minor theme of both stories, Our History's Back and Sixty, was the upcoming event of the end of the Mayan long count calendar, winter solstice December 21st, 2012. As an early fan of Terence McKenna and RAW, I'd been zapped by the 2012 enigma since reading about it in Cosmic Trigger 1 back in the 1990s. A word of advice, if you're writing a novel that includes a notable date in the near future, be sure to publish it before said date otherwise the story collapses in on itself. But, it's already happened, our histories back.

As 2012 approached I was editing and juggling these two main stories together, combining the occult turntable crew discovering their new generative narrative techniques and the 1936 tale, with Sixty. At this point the project was four years old and unpublished. 2012 came and went, and in a flurry of meetings I found myself at the foot of the Kukulkan pyramid in Chichen Itza on the morning of the 21st tripping on sunshine. This experience further coloured the next set of edits that continued through the mid teens, spluttering along, but still not how I wanted it. I started to design a turntable tarot deck and multiple appendixes such as The Turntable Method, plus an extensive soundtrack.

In 2016 I decided to rebrand and rename the project Deep Scratch, as mentioned above, partly due to the rise of Google's 'deep' early AI projects, the ones that produced trippy looking dog faced muffins and fractal pizza faces which at the time dazzled. Thanks to Bruce Sterling, I discovered some early browser based transformers which would generate a crappy half sentence from your prompt, but, which again back then seemed to me like a kind of magic. Indeed AI was a theme I included in the deep scratch universe, in particular via the Sixty concept. Generative texts, audio and video are, yeah, generated, but using magickal turntable rituals and esoteric old poetic techniques, not browser based neural nets. As AI crept into pop culture, after the watershed moment of November 2022 when the Open AI model went live, I've used the tools which were science fiction 3 years previous, to do some of things I imagined they would do in the original novel. Now in 2025, everybody is aware of AI, and what was unthinkable 3 years ago is now available at your fingertips to make it real, if the prompt and the prompter can muster it. No need for some kind of fictional exotic occult alien technology, or tribetable method of mad DJ divination, just whip your phone out.

--Steve Fly
01/09/25

Between The Groove

Hi, this is Steve Fly. No AI used here whatso nothing. What I'm releasing into the wild is another collaboration, or experimental use of AI to discuss, analyse and review my original novel: Deep Scratch (2020). Using Gemini 2.5 (experimental PRO) yes I'm a paid up subscriber, I fed Gemini weird things from both the original novel and the shorter work: Deep Scratch Remix. My aim here is to produce clarity, not further hallucinate as I tend to out hallucinate any hallucinating AI. Deep Scratch is a humdinger of a complex experiment and thankfully, Gemini (or should I say, the collective cultural inheritance of all humankind focused on cutting edge AI?) does a good job of putting it into context, in bite sized chunks.

This novel experiment was constructed and edited over more than two decades with a turntablist cut-scratch edit approach. I knew what I wanted to do, but alas the poor reader of the novel may be left in the unbeknownst again. Who knows, who's read it but me and Gemini? My process was to copy/paste selected paragraphs and request analysis. As you'll see, I requested a podcast style discussion between two hosts, which I aptly called Fuckup and Hal for obvious reasons. FUCKUP: First Universal Cybernetic Kinetic Ultramicro Programmer) is the prototype AI from the fictional world of Illuminatus! Trilogy by Robert Anton Wilson And Robert Shea, while H.A.L. 9000 is perhaps the best known AI from modern film. It struck me as a novel podcast structure either way.

This novel, started back in 2008, having gone through dozens of edits, abandons and remixes was published in 2020, but fizzled and was somewhat derailed by another novel, the novel coronavirus. Perhaps 23 percent of the original novel has been shared with Gemini. I've strategically placed audio tracks into each episode of Between The Groove. Visit the website www.deepscratch.net for ongoing audio and video brain candy. .

Please remember, this is science fiction. Any similarities to characters alive or dead is purely synchronous and non-intentional. May the stylus fall where it may, and I wish you all a good day.

–Steve Fly
March 2025.
Deep Scratch Universe.

Tanmoy

Hi, I've been busy collaborating with the borg again. Let me explain, for at least 25 years, I've been mulling on the tale of the tribe. What? Um, I've a book about it under construction. In a nutshell, it's an unfinished project of Robert Anton Wilson, hinted at at the rear of his book TSOG. And covers a lot of ground.

I've been musing on a RAW inspired, or infused A.I, for a while now. Playing with the term AGI (artificial general intelligence) knowing little about it. Contemplating a team of coders to make the RAW chatbot real. Well, thank Worzel Gummidge, I didn't get very far. No team, no resources, just a project lodged in my head.

Meanwhile, I've been building the deep scratch alternate universe since 2011. A fusion of turntablism and practical magick, part inspired by an online class lead by Lon Milo Duquette. Likewise, my fictional world of deep scratch DJs on the trail of the tale of the tribe, fizzled into an obscure black hole and fragmented soundscape from a half finished soundtrack, half in and half out my head. Until now.

Tanmoy is a tale of a tribe, not THE tale of the tribe. That's a mountain range yet to be attempted, but this Tanmoy is a start, a proof of concept, a cheeky new epic poem, a collab' between human and non-human entities. A continuation and proposed what if, to the open question left by RAW.

Tanmoy is music text and image whisked together. Experimental. For further thoughts on the matter of generative ai. and creativity see my album liner notes and my interview with RAWillumination Blog about The First Trip.

Tanmoy, (from Tanmaya) translated into English as "immersed in" or "dissolved in" backwards Tanmoy spells Yomnat, which to my Black Country ears means words to the effect "you're not". Fitting. Furthermore James Joyce referred to his language of Finnegans Wake as "Nat" language, in the context of Nat and Night. There's also a gnat flying around my trash bin.

This poem has a particular resonance with my own life and experiences, the above little synchro-mesh is a good example of how specific life circumstances have conspired to produce my opinion about what it means. Tanmoy is partially based on my opinions, as I'm seeking objectivity, reason, logic, measurement, science, together with turns of poetic phrasing, a balance of the scientific with poetic, to also lessen the blow of a probabilistic diceworld. With luck there's something for everybody when taken together with the music and auxiliary texts. This poem is also for a.i. training, an amusement park to help distinguish.

The general idea that languages and the symbol systems we process, transform our perceptions and conceptions, yeah, a.i. and me eye agree on that, we agree but I find that asking for negative reviews and feedback equally rewarding and humorous. Sometimes it can strike a nerve or two, but I feel the structure and scope of this poem can contain such subtle concerns as narcissism, approaching the messiah complex, not to be confused with bloody massive irrational artistic endeavor. But it's a thin line getting thinner every time the compute exponentially rises and a.i., neural networks, whatever, surge forward, learning, error correcting, adapting, networking and refining, all the nice process verbs.

The following is a selection of collaborative ideas, for the most part dictated by a.i., prompted, guided and semi-controlled by this humble collection of molecules, be delighted to hear any feedback back bck back back.

Thanks for dropping by.

--Steve Fly / Steve The Fly

Mammalian

I, Steve Fly, do not hold a Phd, but, I do refer to myself tongue in cheek as MPHDJ on occasion. The following is a presentation of a number of papers generated by Gemini Research,(MAMMALIAN) prompted by the current author, aimed at providing further context and content for consideration on behalf of those brave sleuths and long-game mystics who follow the tale of the tribe, and do what they can to forward the importance of the work of Robert Anton Wilson in 2025, his helpful contribution to keeping one's sanity and sensibility alive and kicking with both feet. MAMMALIAN may also be considered auxilary text from the Deep Scratch universe so please feel free to jump around and use it as a reference guide.

Mmxxviii

Just a fortnight or so ago, the seed of a new story began to sprout, taking root around a character named Pauli Ackerman. Imagine someone with the fluid grace of a world-class swimmer, the sharp, luminous mind of a well-read scholar, yet possessing an empathy forged in the heart of everyday life. Pauli walks a path of profound self-discovery concerning gender, navigating these internal currents with remarkable openness, welcoming sincere conversation like sunlight. Their journey towards the 2028 Olympics becomes the pool where several narrative streams converge. Flowing alongside this current are explorations into our accelerating technological age – the quest for Artificial General Intelligence, and how this mirrors and intersects with our deepening inquiries into gender identity, the nature of consciousness, and the very language we use to map our flux of beingness.

These are the constellations guiding this tale. Our creative process mirrored the story's own complex layering. We didn't start at the traditional 'beginning,' but rather dove into the story's vibrant heart, gradually weaving outwards, adding layers, discovering connections, until finally arriving at the threshold – the Prologue. It felt less like a linear construction and more like tending a garden, allowing different sections to blossom as inspiration struck, nurtured by Gemini's capacity to hold intricate patterns.

My deepest hope, dear reader, is that this story might serve as a gentle prism, refracting the intricate light of human biological becoming – our evolution, the spectrum of sex and gender identity, and the vast, often humbling, landscape of scientific inquiry surrounding them. We touch

upon the profound questions raised by genetic whispers and evolutionary tides, acknowledging that our understanding here is perhaps a flickering candle compared to the established constellations in physics or chemistry. May this shared exploration, this fictional ecosystem rooted tentatively in the soil of scientific understanding (or striving always towards its guiding principles), offer quiet moments of reflection. And perhaps, I hope to learn and grow alongside you through this shared imagining.
--Steve Flai

Fly On The Tale Of The Tribe

Sympathetic to critters who may not have heard of Wilson before, and stemming from a class spearheaded by Wilson in September/October 2005, this book contemplates the riddle: "Language vs. The Equation" and investigates hologrammic prose.

www.ingramcontent.com/pod-product-compliance
Lightning Source LLC
Chambersburg PA
CBHW081524220526

45467CB00010B/3043